TOK SEN

Sacred tapping on the Thai meridians

ELEFTERIA MANTZOROU

Contents

FOREWORD

I am very glad I finally managed to write this book! It is based on the techniques we have been demonstrating in FLOW, my little massage therapy school which is located in Athens, Greece.

I learned Tok Sen in Chiang Mai, Thailand. Hence, this book is written with the deepest respect to my Thai instructors, especially the staff of Hang Dong Thai Massage school, where I did my main training in Tok Sen.

Feel free to incorporate these techniques in your massage practice. I hope you will find them beneficial!

WHAT IS TOK SEN?

Tok Sen is an ancient Thai treatment. It is practiced mainly in Northern Thailand, as it originates from *Lanna* traditions. It is performed with a set of wooden tools, which consists of a "hammer" and a "chisel". Both tools bear Buddhist mantras, and have been traditionally blessed by a monk. This blessing is a prerequisite of Tok Sen therapy, otherwise we are talking about two ordinary wooden massage tools, which cannot and should not be named "Tok Sen".

The therapist taps the Thai meridians, which are known as *Sen*, with these tools. It is believed that the blessings of the monk and the sacred vibration of the mantra, are "carried" in the receiver's body via the tapping.

Tok Sen can be seen as a ritual. In Northern Thailand, I have seen Thai therapists reciting mantras while holding the Tok Sen set of tools, and then blowing on them, in order to "infuse" them with the spirit of the invoked deity.

Of course, Tok Sen has also been practised by rural people in Northern Thailand, as a simple type of therapy for muscle aches. This can be done either in the spirit of the ritualistic practices that are followed in places like Chiang Mai, or just as a plain and easy, non-specialized treatment.

Today, Tok Sen is very popular in Northern Thailand, especially around Chiang Mai. I have never seen it in the Southern part of the country, not even in Bangkok. Tok Sen is a service of many spas and massage centers around Chiang Mai and Chiang Rai. Currently, it is even being offered in a Wat (a Thai temple) in Chiang Mai, namely in Wat Mahawan, since it is anyway considered a type of spiritual practice.

The Thai people have incorporated in their religion and spiritual life numerous pre-Buddhist animist practices, which are called *Satsana Phi*. Tok Sen can be considered a practice which is performed in the context of *Satsana Phi*.

The Tok Sen tapping can be performed in a few different ways, from what I have observed in Northern Thailand. The differences have to do with the number of times of the tapping on the same point, as well as with the speed of application (ok, obviously there are innumerable variations to that!).

Tok Sen is usually performed within the context of a traditional Thai Massage technique. It is been taught in many massage schools in and around Chiang Mai.

The Lanna Kingdom

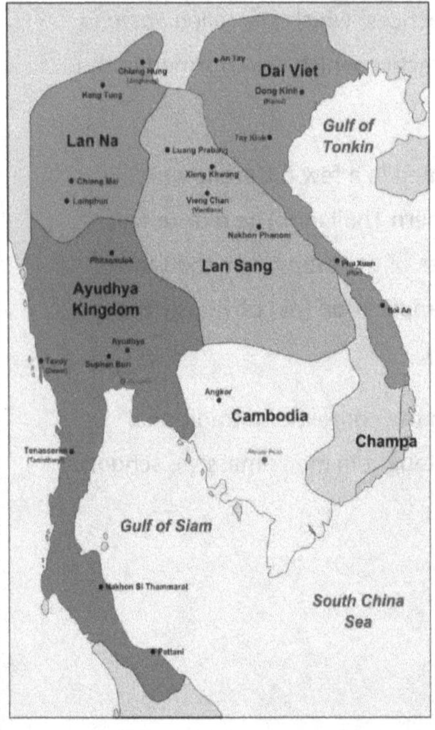

1. Lanna Kingdom[1].

The Lanna Kingdom (meaning "Kingdom of a Million Rice Fields"), also known as *Lannathai* or *Lan Na*, was an Indianized state centered in present-day Northern Thailand, from the 13th to 18th centuries.

The cultural development of the Northern Thai people had begun long before as successive kingdoms preceded Lan Na.

The kings of Lan Na states remained faithful to the Chakri Dynasty of Siam, who provided them with protection against Burma. By 1909, Lanna Kingdom no longer existed formally as Siam finalized the demarcation of its borders with the British and French; Lanna Kingdom was then recognized as a part of Thailand and not as an independent entity[i].

Chiang Mai was the Kingdom's capital from 1292 until 1775.

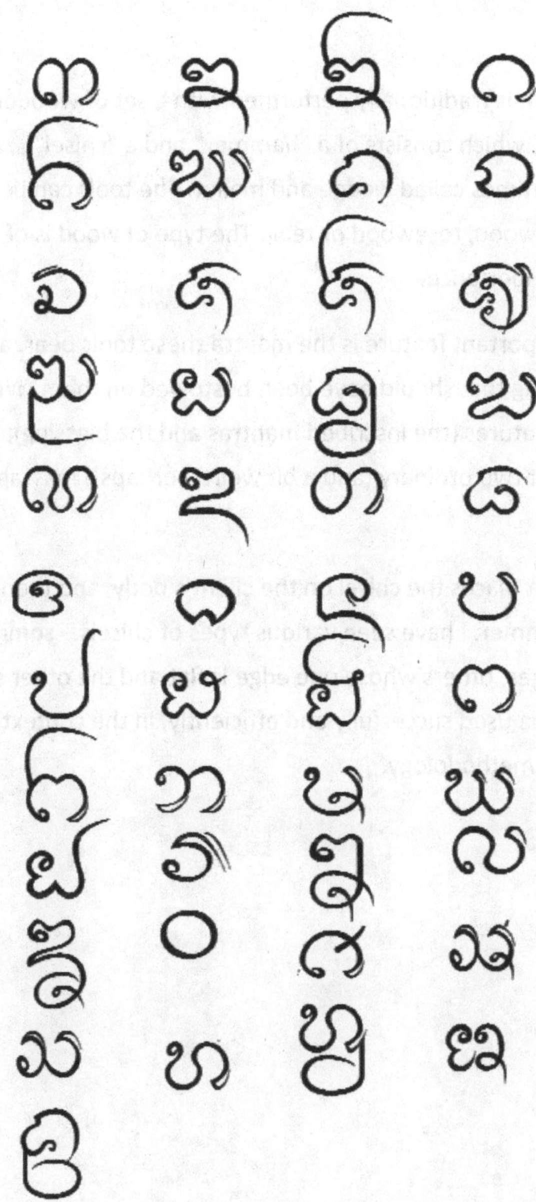

2. The forty-four consonants of the Lanna abugida (alphasyllabary)[ii].

THE TOK SEN TOOLS

Tok Sen is traditionally performed with a set of wooden tools, which consists of a "hammer" and a "chisel", sometimes called wedge and mallet. The tools can be made of tamarind wood, rosewood or teak. The type of wood is of secondary importance.

The most important feature is the mantra these tools bear, as well as the blessing that should have been bestowed on them. Without these two features (the inscribed mantras and the blessing), we are talking about two ordinary (and a bit weird perhaps!) massage tools.

The therapist places the chisel on the client's body, and then taps it with the hammer. I have seen various types of chisels – some with rounded edges, others whose one edge is flat and the other sharp etc. All can be used succesfully and efficiently, in the context of the appropriate methodology.

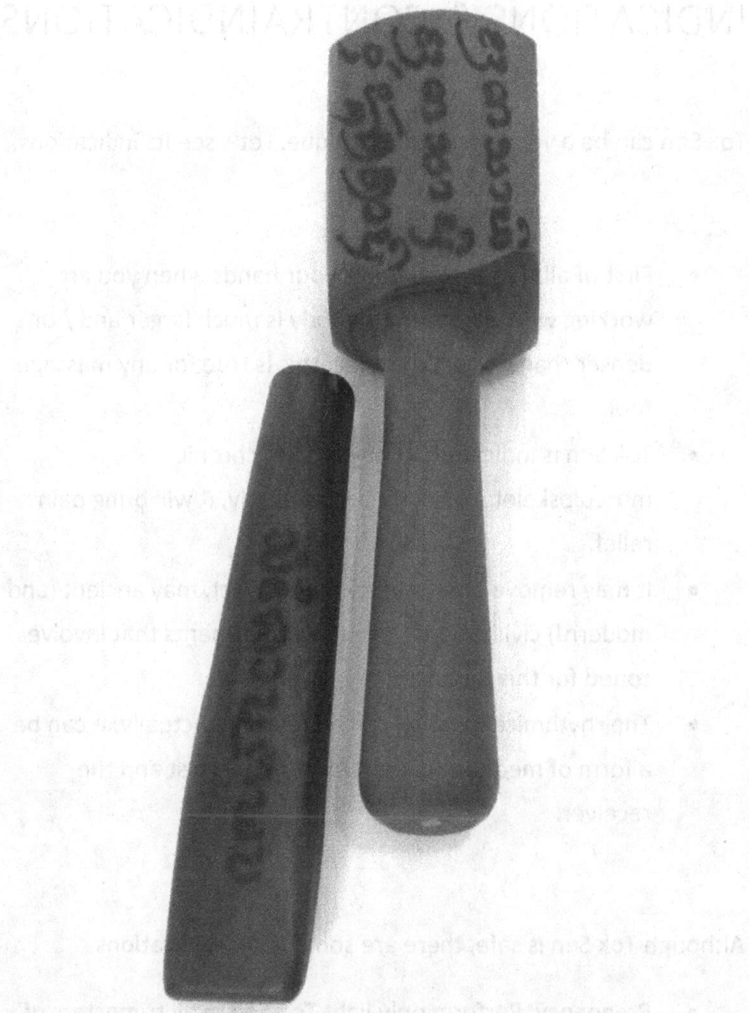

3. A typical Tok Sen set, consisting of a "chisel" (left), and a "hammer" (right).

INDICATIONS & CONTRAINDICATIONS

Tok Sen can be a very effective technique. Let's see its indications.

- First of all, Tok Sen can save your hands when you are working with clients whose body is much larger and / or denser than yours. Of course, this is true for any massage tool.
- Tok Sen is indicated for any type of chronic musculoskeletal pain. If used correctly, it will bring pain relief.
- It may remove energy blockages. In fact, may ancient (and modern!) civilizations have used treatments that involve sound for this purpose.
- The rhythmical tapping can be relaxing. Actually, it can be a form of meditation, both for the therapist and the receiver.

Although Tok Sen is safe, there are some contraindications.

- Pregnancy. Perform only light Tok Sen in all trimesters of pregnancy. Avoid it altogether on the belly and the hamstrings.
- Fever – even low-grade fever. Tok Sen will stimulate the blood flow, and thus worsen any fever and / or infection.
- Tok Sen should not be performed on patients with tumors.

- Do not perform Tok Sen on patients who have had a cardiac arrest within the previous six months, without the doctor's approval.

- Acute inflammation of the musculoskeletal system is an absolute contraindication.

- Do not perform Tok Sen on burns, and on any inflamed area of the skin.

- Tok Sen is contraindicated in patients who have spider veins, varicose veins and any large, raised, swollen blood vessels. This is a local contraindication, unless there is a blood clot or an aneurysm.

- It may not be advisable to perform Tok Sen on people who are stout followers of a religion which disapproves of spiritual treatments of the East.

If you have any doubts about the suitability of Tok Sen for a client, please consult his or her doctor.

FREQUENTLY ASKED QUESTIONS ABOUT TOK SEN

Is Tok Sen painful?

Tok Sen is NOT painful. It appears so, but it is not. Sometimes, a technique that appears in a video or in a photo, may give an entirely different impression than its actual feeling.

That being said, Tok Sen can be dangerous if a powerful hit is applied on bones, or at the origin or insertion of a muscle.

Is Tok Sen performed directly on skin?

Tok Sen can be performed either directly on the skin, or above thin clothing. Personally, I prefer to apply it directly on the skin. In this book, I demonstrate the techniques above clothing.

Oh, an important thing: Do not use any oils while performing Tok Sen. It is a dry massage technique.

Tok Sen is applied only within the context of Thai Massage?

Yes, usually it is applied by a therapist who has been trained in Thai Massage. However, it is a simple technique, and it can be applied by any properly trained massage therapist who respects its tradition. Tok Sen is usually applied on the Sen lines of Thai medicine, but a therapist who is not trained in that can also use a musculoskeletal approach.

Is there a traditional script on Tok Sen?

Sadly no. At least there is not one that I am aware of. Tok Sen has been mostly preserved as an oral tradition in Northern Thailand.

Do I have to become a Buddhist in order to perform Tok Sen?

Not really. I do not consider myself a Buddhist (actually I am not a follower of any religion, although I do consider myself a spiritual person and I do believe in a higher power in the universe), but I perform Tok Sen. But if you really dislike Buddhism or the indigenous Thai traditions, it is better not to do it, as there is a spiritual dimension to it.

Can I just use my hammer???

Feel free to use any tools in your massage practice — I use my dough roller sometimes - but Tok Sen is a different story. As it was said earlier, what makes Tok Sen special, is the spiritual blessing of the tools.

4. Tok sen tools, and Thai herbal ball ingredients, at the Hang Dong Thai Massage school.

5. The altar where the Tok Sen tools are blessed. Hang Dong Thai Massage school, Chiang Mai.

SIP SEN – THE TEN LINES

In the Thai language, sen means "line". The Thai meridians are called Sen, and in massage therapy, ten basic "lines" are used (sip means "ten").

The sen have more similarities with the Ayurvedic nadi, than with the Chinese meridians. The sen do not correspond to specific organs, like the Chinese meridians, and are indicated for problems that may occur across their course. Each sen has some acupressure points.

Sen work is called jap sen, and it is done in 5 steps, in Thai Massage:

- Stretching (opening the line)
- Walking with palms (warming the line)
- Walking with thumbs (working on specific lines and points)
- Walking with palms (warming the line)
- Stretch (opening the line).

According to the traditional protocol, the therapist should start working upwards all sen lines – that is, from the feet towards the head, and from the hands towards the heart. Then, he should return to the starting point. Bear in mind that there may be some differences to this protocol, depending on the school.

It is not necessary to work all the lines in one session, and it is not necessary to work on the whole course of a line.

Jap sen should be applied after training with a qualified teacher.

There are many sen lines crossing the legs. There are three lines on the outer surface of the leg, and 3 in the interior.

These are the lines that run on the outer leg:

1st line: Itha or Pingkala
2nd line: Sahatsarangsi or Tawaree
3rd line: Itha or Pingkala

These are the lines that run on the inner leg:

1st line: Sahatsarangsi or Tawaree
2nd line: Kalatharee
3rd line: Itha or Pingkala

My instructors in Thailand used to say that a Sen line can have one of three colors: white (corresponds to nerves), red (corresponds to arteries), or black (corresponds to veins).

Work on the Sen lines can be used to "open" deeper levels of the body. According to Thai medicine, the human body has five levels:

1. Epidermis (the top layer of the skin).
2. Subcutaneous tissue (also known as the hypodermis or superficial fascia).
3. Sen lines
4. Bones
5. Organs

Now, let's have a look at the Sen lines – the Thai meridians.

1, 2. Itha & Pingkala sen

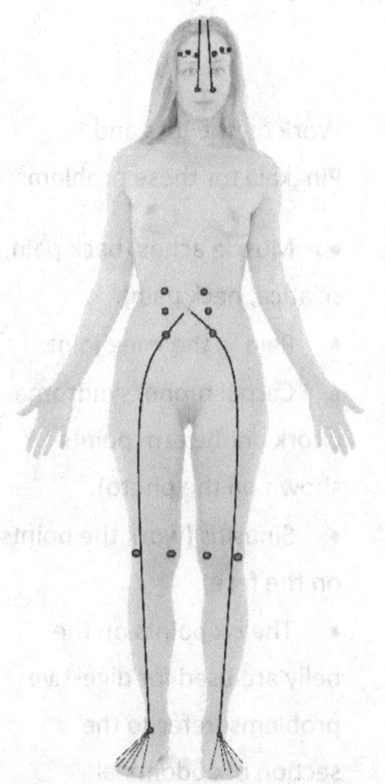

Itha originates from the navel and descends the anterior part of the left thigh, forming the first external line. Then it turns outwards on the left knee, and then follows an upward course between the heads of the posterior thigh muscles, forming the third inner line. It continues its course next to the spine, passes from the scalp and the forehead, and finally ends on the left nostril.

Pingkala follows the same path, but on the right part of the body.

These meridians also have sub-branches.

There is a sub-branch that continues until the toes of the dorsal aspect of the foot, and another that run between the heads of the gastrocnemius muscle (starts below the knee joint).

Also, in the upper part of the thoracic spine, there is another sub-branch, which passes next to the scapula, crosses the anterior surface of the arm and

the dorsal surface of the hand, and ends on the fingertips.

Finally, there is a sub-branch above each eyebrow.

Another sub-branch starts from the hip bone and runs down to the ankle, forming the third outer energy line of the leg.

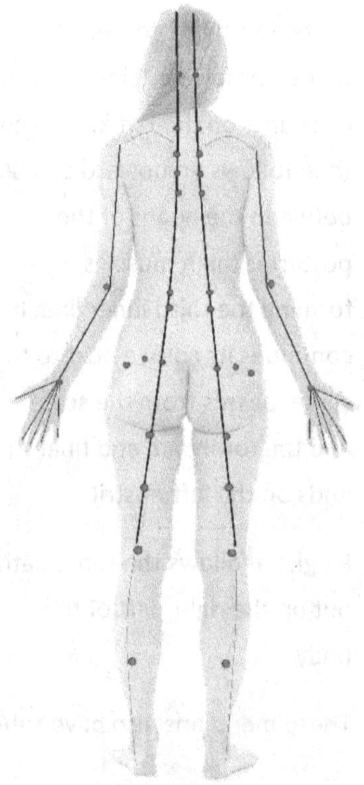

Work on the Itha and Pingkala for these problems:

- Muscle aches (back pain, sciatica, neck pain).
- Pain in the knee joint.
- Carpal tunnel syndrome (work on the arm points shown on the photo).
- Sinusitis (work the points on the face).
- The six points on the belly are used for digestive problems (refer to the section of abdominal techniques for the procedure), and for lower back pain.

These sen are connected to the sense of smell.

3. Sumana Sen

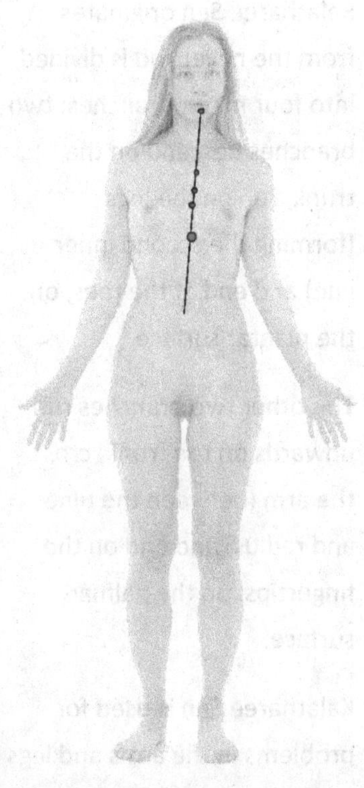

Sumana Sen originates from the navel, crosses the trunk, and ends at the root of the tongue. It is connected to the sense of taste.

Work on Sumana Sen for disorders related to the respiratory system, and the mind (stress, arrhythmias, etc).

The point below the xiphoid process is used for digestive disorders (dyspepsia, gastroesophageal reflux, etc.)

The points on the sternum are used for breathing problems.

The point below the lips is used for nausea.

The point at the root of the tongue is only used when we want to eliminate some toxic substance from the body via emesis. In order to activate it, the finger is inserted into the oral cavity (needless to say, never do this at a client!).

4. Kalatharee Sen

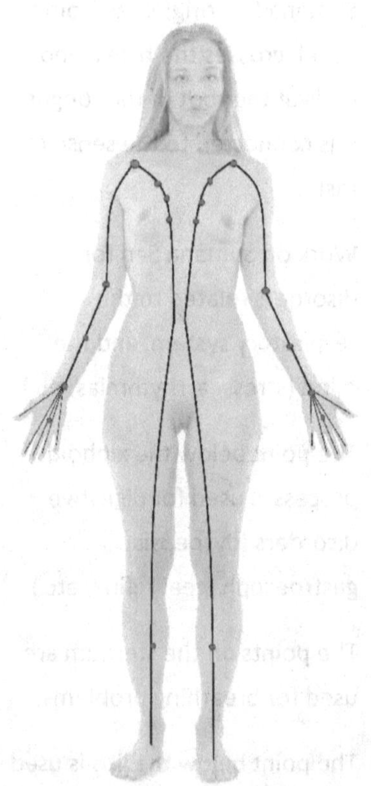

Kalatharee Sen originates from the navel and is divided into four major branches: two branches descend on the trunk, run on the legs (forming the second inner line) and end at the toes, on the plantar surface.

The other two branches run upwards on the trunk, cross the arm (between the ulna and radius) and end on the fingertips, on the palmar surface.

Kalatharee Sen is used for problems in the arms and legs (pain, weakness, numbness, muscle aches, etc.). However, it is also the main sen indicated for arrhythmias and disorders of the nervous system.

Kalatharee Sen is connected to the sense of touch.

The points of the legs are shown in the illustration.

One is located three fingers below the knee, while the other is next to the ankle.

Points on the arms and hands:

- The first point of the arm is lateral and superior to the sternum at the lateral side of the first intercostal space.
- There is a second point, located in the center of the arm.
- The third point is located is located on the transverse crease of the elbow, and it is indicated for tennis elbow.
- The fourth point is located at the center of the forearm.
- There is also a fifth point on the wrist joint, in the middle of the transverse crease of the wrist. It is indicated for wrist pain, and also for stress and palpitations.

5, 6. Sahatsarangsi & Tawaree Sen

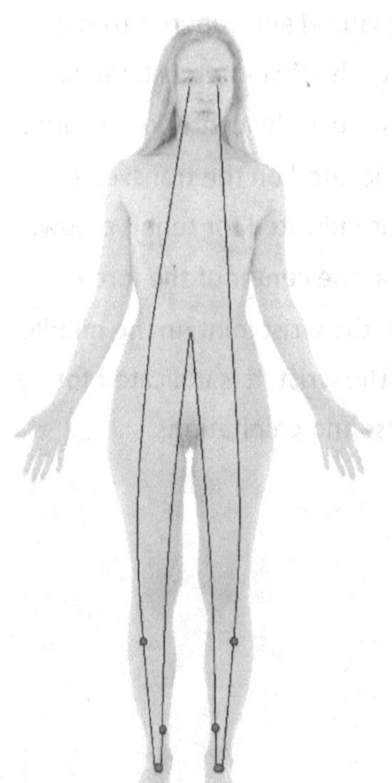

Sahatsarangsi Sen originates from the navel, descends at the inner surface of the left leg, forming the first inner line. Then it turns on the left ankle, forming the second outer line, and runs upwards to the neck. It ends below the left eye.

Tawaree Sen follows the same path, but on the right part of the body.

Both Sen are connected to the sense of sight.

These two sen are used for leg and eye problems. If there is an eye problem, work on the sen that runs on the opposite leg (e.g. if there is a problem on the left eye, work on Tawaree sen).

The first point is located is located four finger widths down from the bottom of the patella, along the outer boundary of the shin bone. Use it for pain on the legs.

The second point is on the dorsum of the foot, at the midpoint of the transverse crease of the ankle joint. It is indicated for ankle pain.

7. Nantakawat Sen

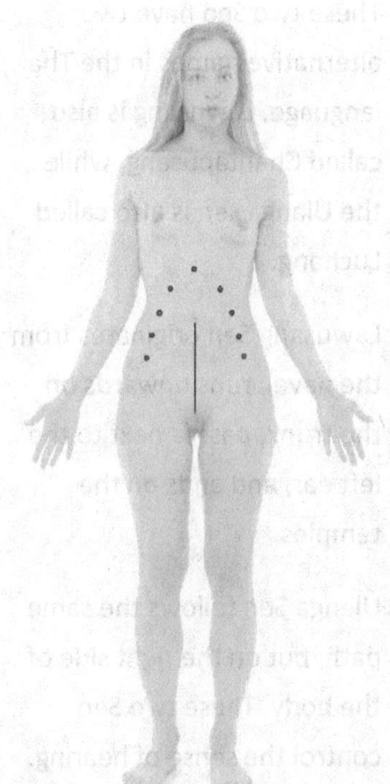

Nantakawat Sen originates from the navel and is divided into two branches.

The first is called Sukumang and ends at the anus, while the second is called Sikinee and ends at the urethra.

This Sen controls the absorption of food, the transformation of liquids and the elimination of waste substances from the body.

Nantakawat Sen is mainly associated with the processes of urination and defacation.

Generally, it is used for digestive problems (constipation, irritable bowel syndrome, etc.).

In cases of constipation work in a clockwise direction, while in cases of diarrhea work anticlockwise, on the 9 points shown on the illustration.

8, 9. Lawusang & Ulanga Sen

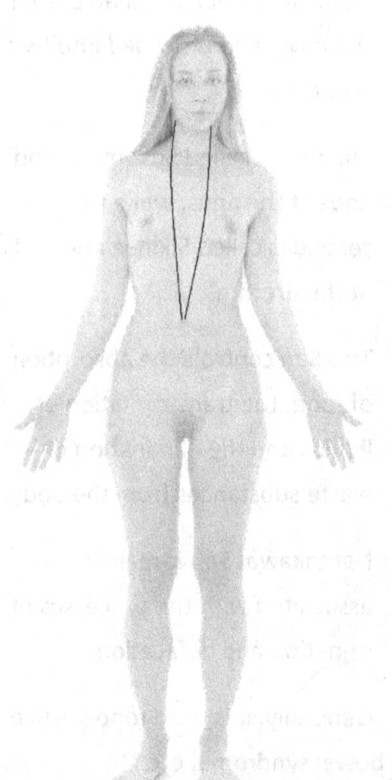

These two Sen have two alternative names in the Thai language. Lawusang is also called Chantapusang, while the Ulanga sen is also called Luchang.

Lawusang Sen originates from the navel, runs upwards on the trunk, passes next to the left ear, and ends on the temples.

Ulanga Sen follows the same path, but on the right side of the body. These two Sen control the sense of hearing.

Generally, they are used for pain on the face. They can be used for:

- earache and tinnitus (due to stress).
- any pain not due to acute inflammation (e.g. headaches).
- motion sickness.

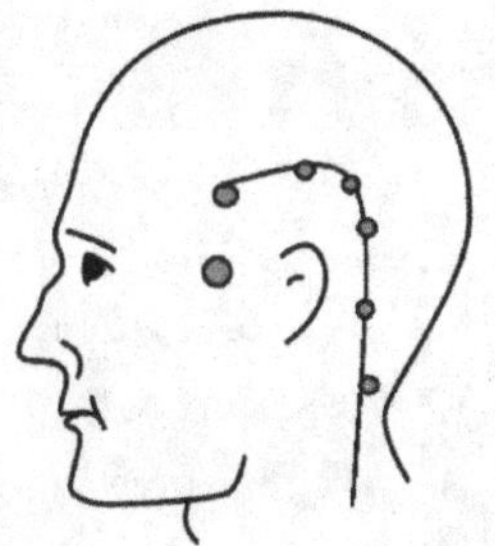

The course of Lawusang and Ulanga Sen around the ear.

10. Kitcha Sen

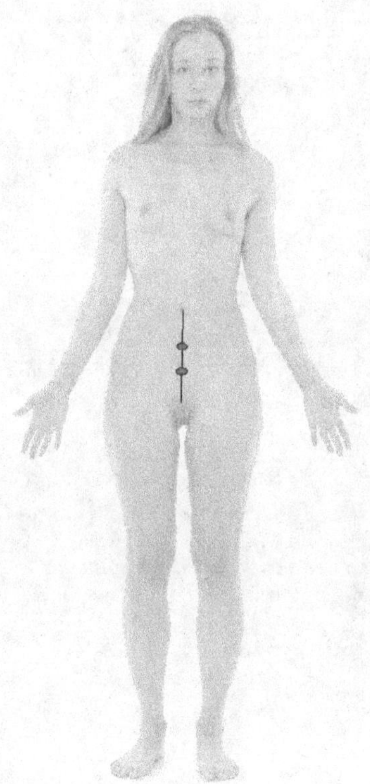

Kitcha Sen originates from the navel and descends to the genitals. In women ends on the clitoris, and is called Kitchana. In men, it reaches the end of the penis, and is called Pittakun.

Generally, it is controls sexual arousal, and reproductive capacity and function. Kitcha Sen is used mainly in cases of sexual frigidity, erectile dysfunction, and also for disorders of the female reproductive system.

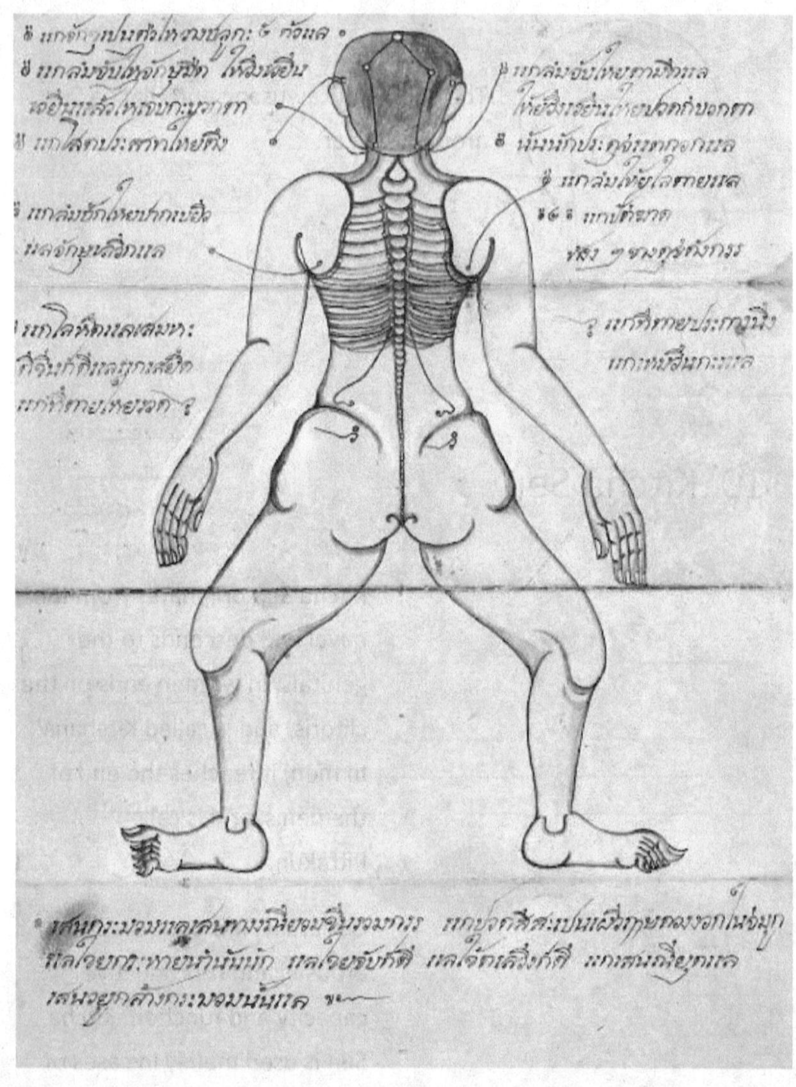

6 . A Traditional Thai medicine plate which depicts acupressure points on Sen lines. Image reproduced with the kind permission of the British Library.

SPACE & HYGIENE

Here are some rules for the area where a Tok Sen session is performed:

• The mat on which we place the receiver should be soft. The mat should be placed on a non-slippery floor or material.

• Have at least 3-4 pillows to support the body of the receiver correctly. It is advisable to have an extra pillow for your knees.

• The therapist and the receiver should wear comfortable, loose clothes.

• The room must be very clean.

• I recommend dim lighting and soothing music.

• The receiver should not have eaten a heavy meal at least two hours before a Tok Sen session. After the session, I tell my clients to avoid food for the next hour, to drink lots of water, and to bathe after 2-3 hours.

• The therapist should wash his / her hands **before** the massage.

• The sheet covering the mattress should be washed after each session. The same applies to the pillow.

> Never wash your Tok Sen tools with soap and water. Place them in a UV sanitizer, or disinfect them with an antiseptic lotion or wipes.

TOK SEN TECHNIQUES

Tok Sen has two main techniques. For simplicity's sake, I 'll call the first "tapping", and the second "feather tapping". I have never seen these terms anywhere else, I made them up. Feel free to name these techniques as you like.

The tapping technique

In the tapping technique, the therapist taps the Tok Sen tools twice on the same spot, with normal to strong power. This technique is applied on the belly of large muscles, on the back, and next to the scapula.

The tapping technique consists of a double tap, as we said. After the double tap on a spot, the therapist proceeds to apply another double tap 1-2 cm away from the previous spot, and continues in that way across a Sen line or a large muscle.

The feather tapping technique

The feather tapping is applied on the origin and the insertion of muscles, and also on bones. It is also applied on the face. In this technique, the therapist applies swift, very light taps around bony prominences, bones and tendons.

Feather tapping does not consist of a double tap, but of many light taps on an area. It can be a highly skilful technique, and it takes a while to master it. It is not difficult, but takes a bit of practice.

This technique can also be applied on sen lines, on sensitive regions. A good example would be the branch of Itha & Pingkala Sen on the dorsal aspect of the feet, or around the elbow joint.

It is possible to tap on limbs and on the trunk, and then combine tapping with massage techniques, or to follow the "flows" which are demonstrated on page 70 and / or 56.

Watch the video from which this book was created, here: http://bit.ly/toksentherapy

Now, let's see some Tok Sen techniques!

Supine Position

Now, we 'll see some techniques for the supine position. I start from the legs, following the traditional Thai Massage protocol.

THE LEGS

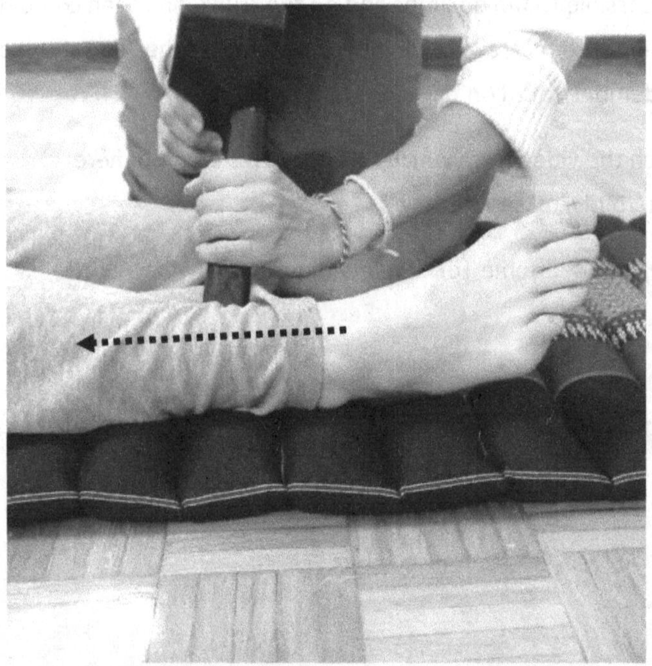

Start from the first inner Sen line, and apply tapping. Begin two inches above the medial malleolus.

A malleolus is the bony prominence on each side of the human ankle. The medial malleolus is the prominence on the inner side of the ankle, formed by the lower end of the tibia.

It is best to sit at the opposite side of the leg you are working on, in order to have better leverage. This will also protect your lower back.

Work with the tapping technique until the lower end of the knee joint, following the first inner Sen line. Then, work downwards until you reach again the medial malleolus, and start tapping the second inner Sen line. Work with tapping on the second inner Sen line until you reach the lower end of the knee joint, and work downwards until you reach again the medial malleolus.

The third inner line is not accessible from the supine position, as it located between the two heads of the gastrocnemius muscle.

When you reach the medial malleolus after having performed tapping on the two inner Sen lines, do feather tapping around the ankle joint.

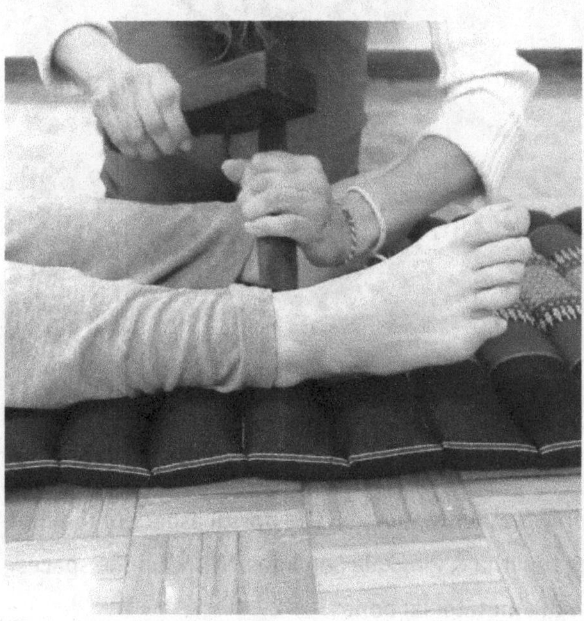

The structures that pass behind medial malleolus deep to the flexor retinaculum are:

- Tibialis posterior tendon
- Flexor digitorum longus
- Posterior tibial artery
- Posterior tibial vein
- Tibial nerve
- Flexor hallucis longus

Thus, the therapist needs to be careful not to damage these delicate structures with strong tapping on this area.

Then, apply feather tapping on the dorsal aspect of the foot, following the Itha & Pingkala Sen lines. Work on the spaces between the metatarsal bones.

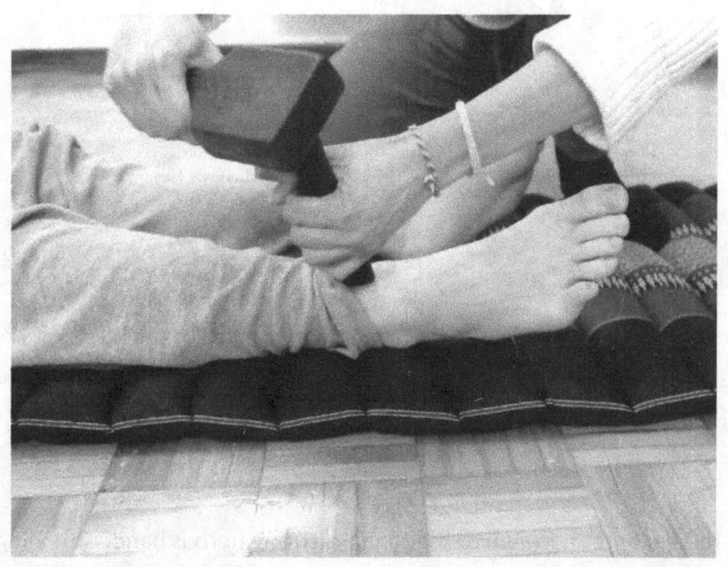

Then, apply feather tapping on the flexor retinaculum, and also between the tibialis anterior and the extensor digitorum longus. Work 4-5 times upwards and downwards on the region.

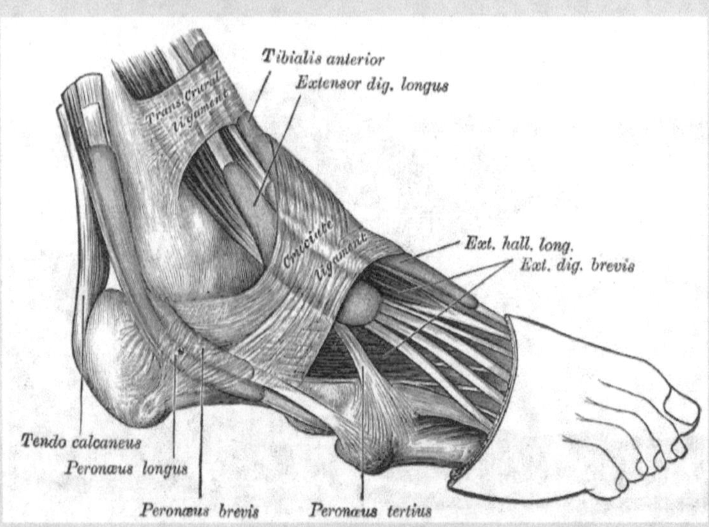

The flexor retinaculum of the foot is a strong fibrous band, extending from the bony ankle prominence (malleolus) above, to the margin of the heelbone (calcaneus) below, converting a series of bony grooves in this situation into canals for the passage of the tendons of the flexor muscles and the posterior tibial vessels and tibial nerve into the sole of the foot.

It is continuous by its upper border with the deep fascia of the leg, and by its lower border with the plantar aponeurosis and the fibers of origin of the abductor hallucis muscle.

Enumerated from the medial side, the four canals which it forms transmit the tendons of the tibialis posterior and flexor digitorum longus muscles; the posterior tibial artery and tibial nerve, which run through a broad space beneath the ligament; and lastly, in a canal formed partly by the talus, the tendon of the flexor hallucis longus[iii].

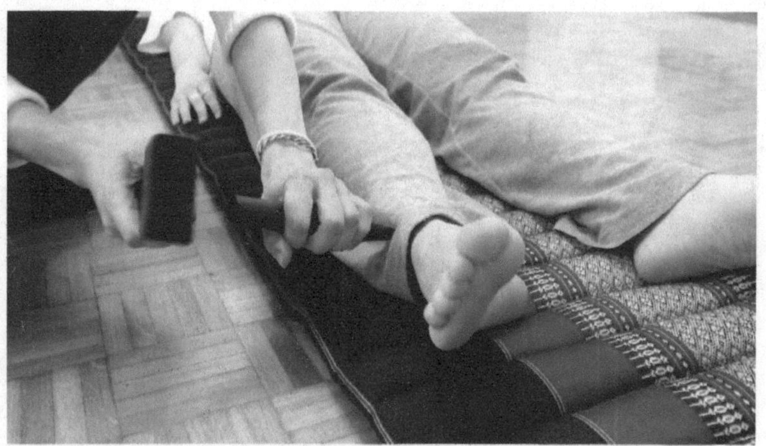

After completing Tok Sen work on the inner lines of the leg, it is time to work on the outer Sen lines of the leg. I use the tapping technique for this.

Start from the first outer line, above the ankle joint. Work until the knee, and then tap again downwards.

Then do tapping on the second Sen line, again starting above the ankle joint. Work until the knee, and then tap again downwards. Repeat the same process on the third Sen line.

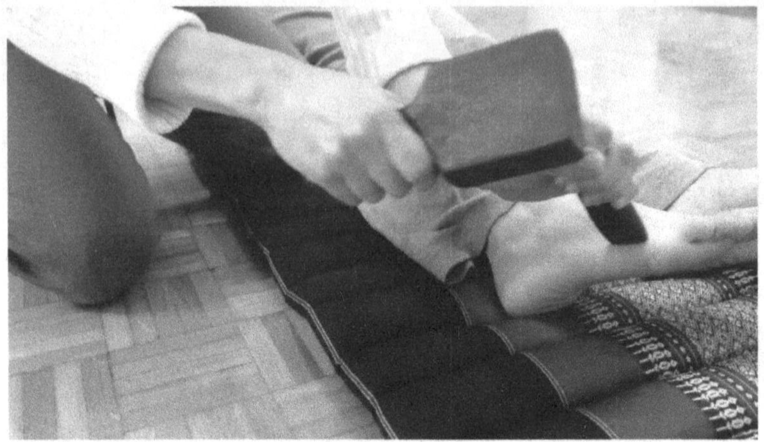

When you reach the ankle joint after tapping upwards and downwards on the third outer Sen line, do some feather tapping on the fifth metatarsal bone and around the ankle.

Then, proceed again upwards, do some feather tapping around the knee joint, and start working on the Sen lines of the thigh.

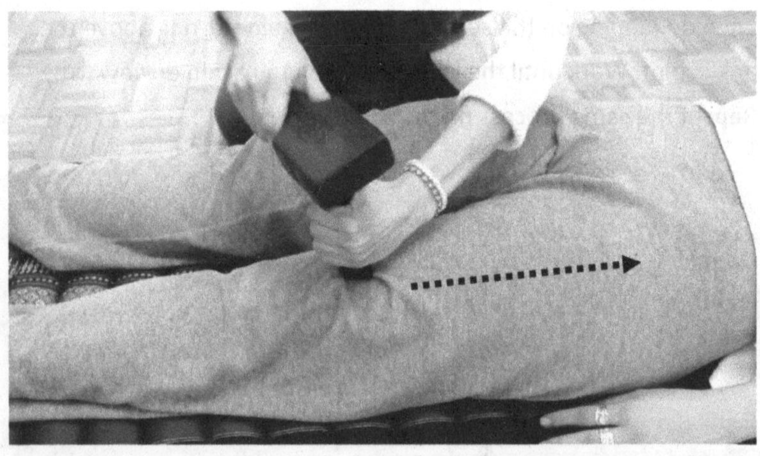

Start above the knee joint and do tapping on the first outer Sen line, towards the trunk.

Stop at the upper part of the quadriceps muscle, and then work again downwards. Repeat the same protocol for the second and third outer Sen lines.

Then, bend the leg, as shown in photo, in order to work on the inner Sen lines.

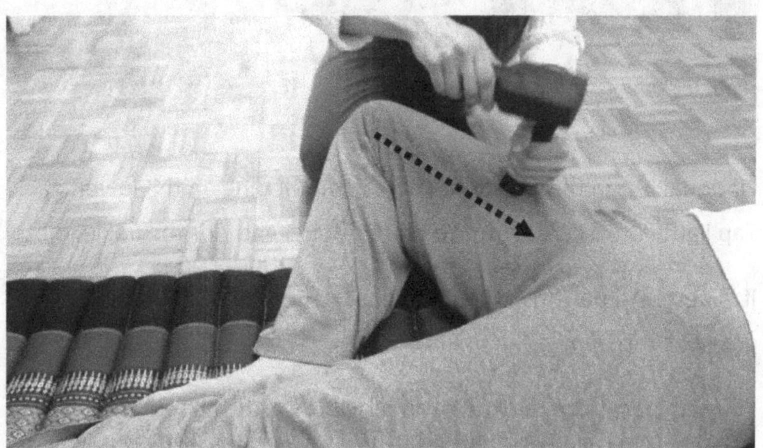

Again, work from the knee joint towards the trunk, and then backwards. Work in this fashion on the first and second inner Sen lines.

It is recommended to place a pillow under the receiver's knee joint.

When you complete your tapping work on the inner Sen lines and you have reached the knee joint, work again upwards on the second inner Sen line with tapping, until the upper part of the quadriceps muscle. Then, do feather tapping on a straight line, until you reach the lower end of the abdominal area.

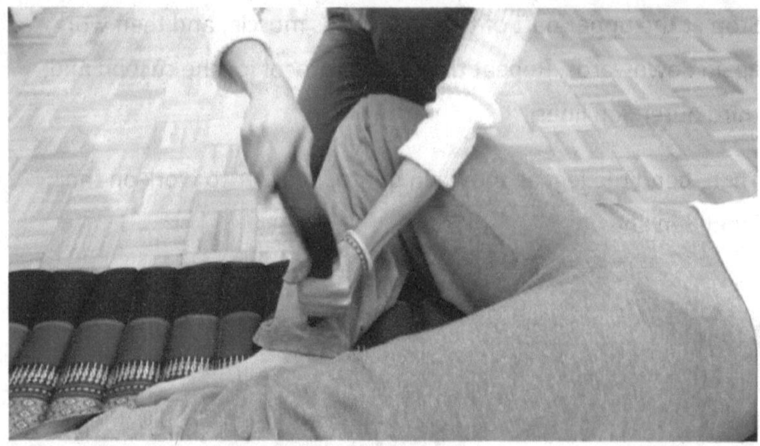

Optional: From this position, you can do tapping on the lower leg. Tap lightly... Be careful not to hit the fibula and / or the ankle joint.

It is better to perform the tapping with the side of the tool, for greater precision.

You can start from the knee and move towards the foot...

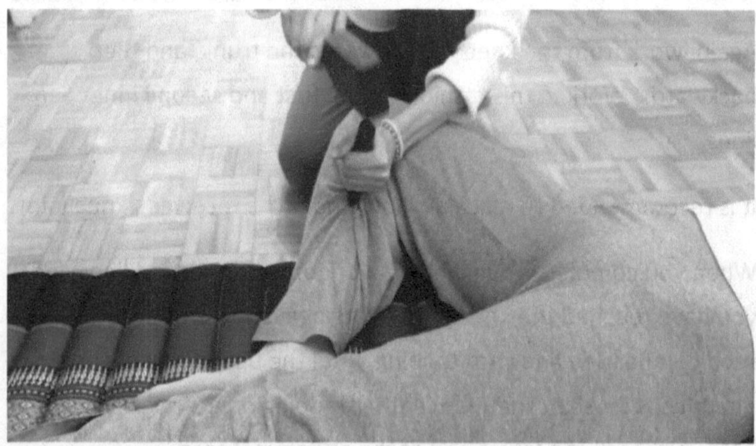

...and then return upwards. Repeat 2-3 times or as needed.

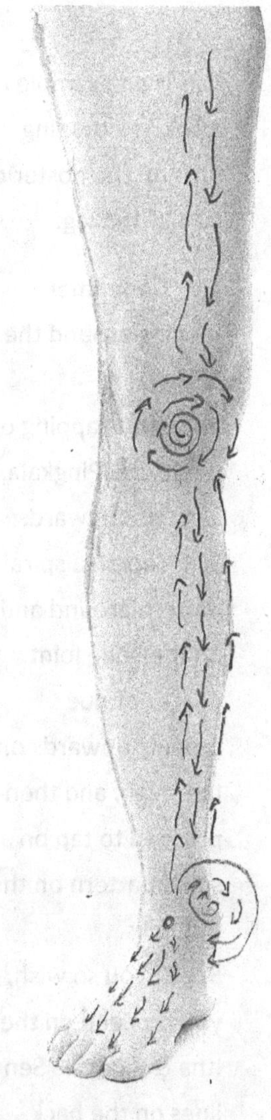

This is an example of a Tok Sen tapping flow on the anterior part of the leg:

1. Do feather tapping on the dorsal aspect of the foot.
2. Start tapping on the Sen lines upward.
3. Tap on a spiral pattern around and on the knee joint.
4. Continue tapping upwards on the thigh, and then proceed downwards.
5. If you so wish, you can tap on more Sen lines on the leg.

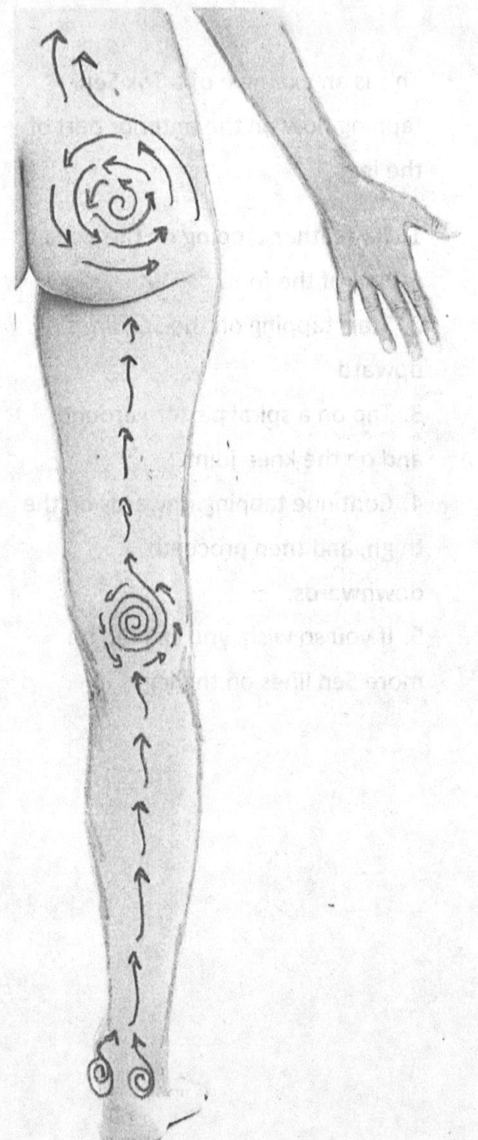

This is an example of a Tok Sen tapping flow on the posterior part of the leg:

1.   Do feather tapping around the ankle joint.
2.   Start tapping on the Itha & Pingkala Sen lines upward.
3.   Tap on a spiral pattern around and on the knee joint.
4.   Continue tapping upwards on the thigh, and then proceed to tap on a spiral pattern on the buttocks.
5.   If you so wish, you proceed on the Itha & Pingkala Sen lines on the back.

THE TRUNK

After having completed Tok Sen work on the legs, it is time to work on the belly. On the abdominal area, apply again the tapping technique, but with much lower intensity.

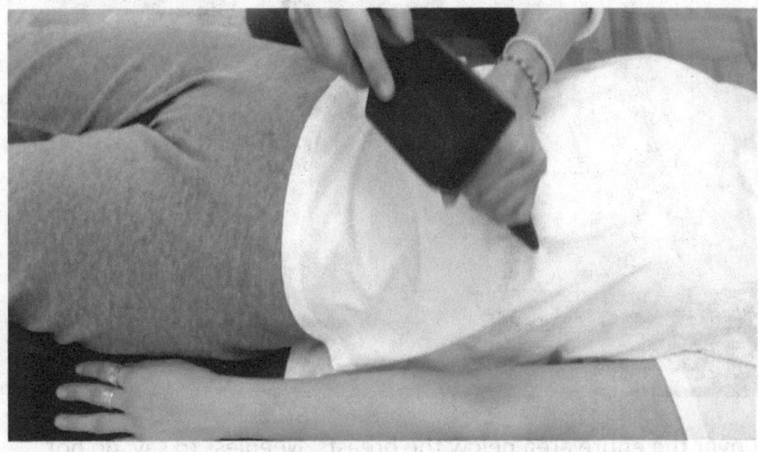

Apply double tapping on the abdominal area, creating a spiral around the umbilicus. I repeat, be gentle on that area.

This technique is indicated for constipation. Since the solar plexus is also located on this region, the technique can also be indicated for emotional blockages.

Working on the ribs and the diaphragm

When you complete your work on the abdominal area, you can work on the ribs. Work only with feather tapping on the ribs.

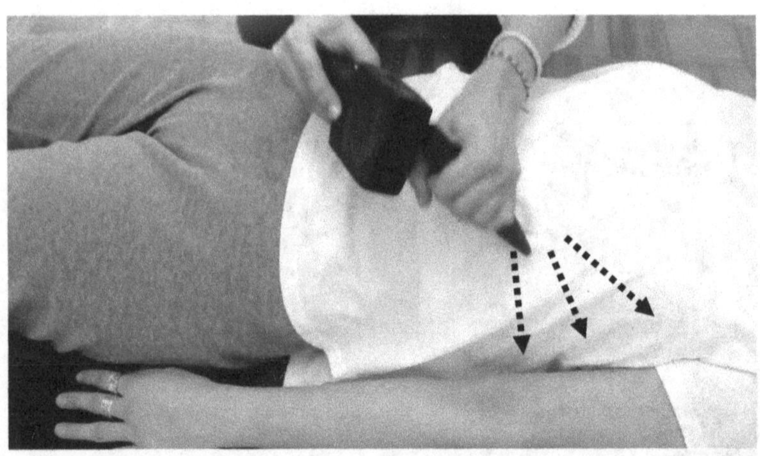

Cover the entire area below the breasts. Needless to say, do not work on the breasts at all! And yes, this would apply for a man as well, for the chest.

When you complete your work on the one side of the body, cover the other side as well. You do not have to move over to the client's other side for that – you can work both sides of the body from the same side.

Feather tapping is also a great technique for the diaphragm. It is indicated especially for people with respiratory ailments. Work 3-4 times on the diaphragm, on each side of the body.

ARMS & HANDS

Tok Sen techniques on the arms and hands can be very relaxing. Although it can be applied by itself, it of course more beneficial when it is combined with the right massage and / or fascia therapy techniques.

Indications include tennis elbow, tired arms, carpal tunnel syndrome and stress.

Arm and hand techniques are generally gentle, and can be applied almost to all age groups. They are indicated especially for neck pain (numbness in the arms originates from the neck, as these areas are connected neurologically), stress, shoulder pain, and of course pain localized on the arm and the hand. They work especially well when combined with warm herbal packs and heat rubs.

The Kalatharee Sen arm branch has a definite connection to the heart, at an energetic level. Thus, work on this sen can be beneficial for arrythmias – especially if they are due to stress.

Work on the Itha & Pingkala Sen branches of the arms and hands is indicated for tendonitis and overuse disorders.

The therapist should be careful not to apply dynamic arm stretches to clients who have had shoulder dislocation, any rotator cuff injury and / or have loose shoulder ligaments or general instability of this area.

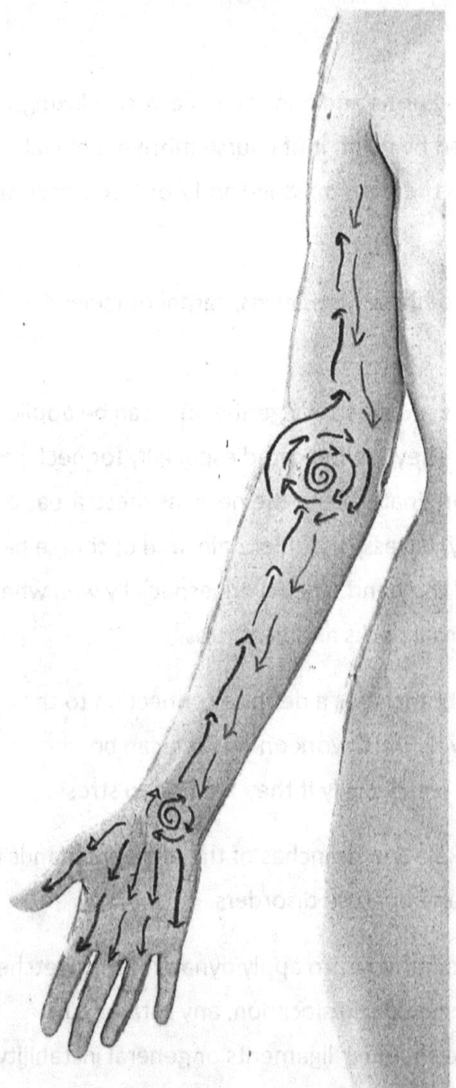

This is an example of a Tok Sen tapping flow on the arm:

1. Do feather tapping on the palm.
2. Start tapping on the Sen lines upwards (Kalatharee Sen at the anterior surface of the arm, Itha & Pingkala Sen at the posterior surface of the arm)..
3. Tap on a spiral pattern around the elbow joint.
4. Continue tapping upwards, and then proceed downwards.

It does not really matter from which side you start – the anterior or the posterior.

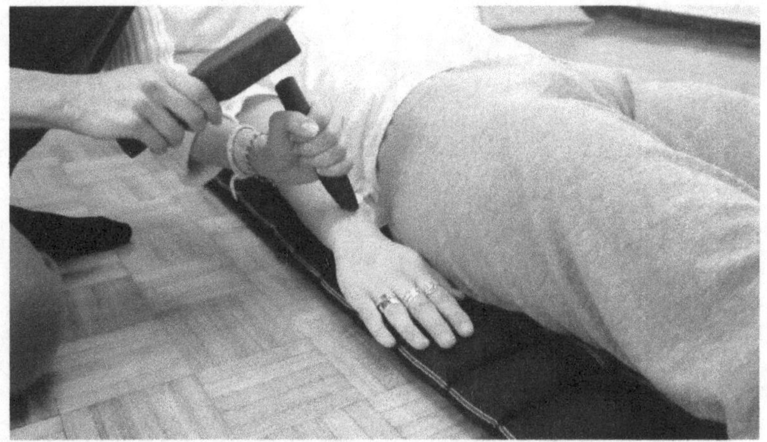

Start by doing tapping on the Itha & Pingkala Sen branches of the arm. The Sen is located between the radius and the ulna. Begin tapping above the wrist, and work upwards towards the elbow joint.

Then, work downwards. Stop before the wrist joint...

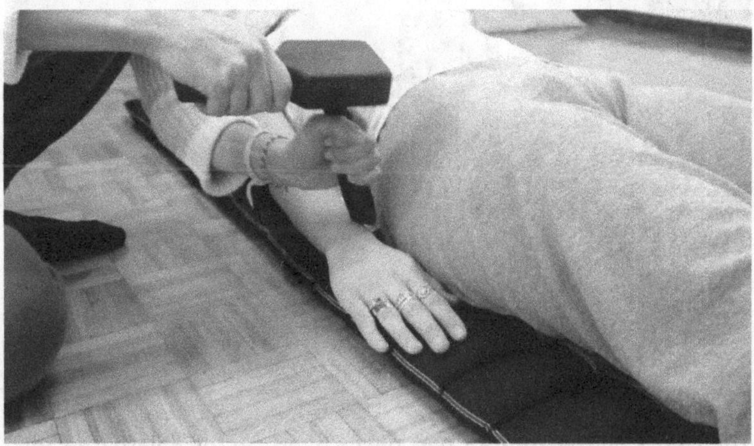

...and do feather tapping on the wrist joint.

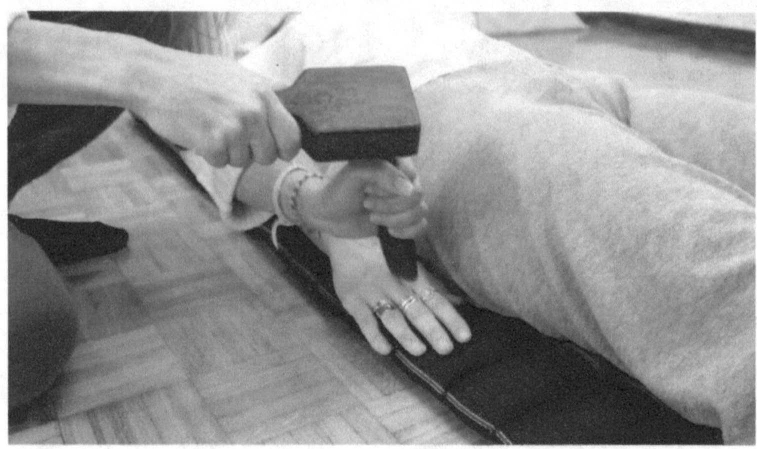

Then, apply feather tapping on the fingers, following the course of Itha & Pingkala Sen on the dorsal aspect of the hand. Work each "line" on the fingers 3-4 times.

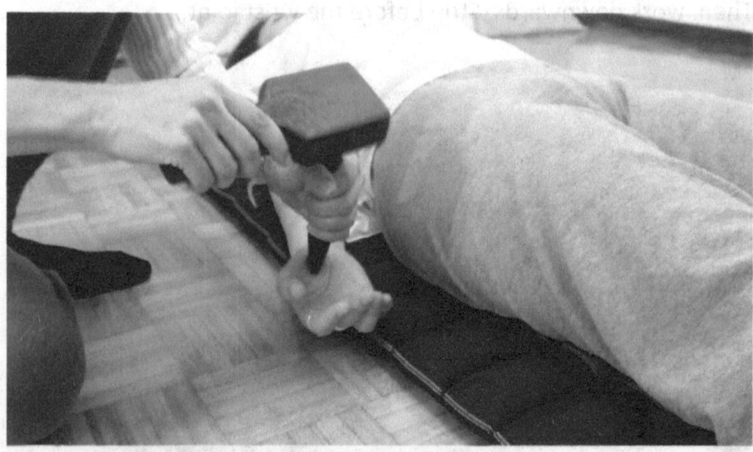

Then work on the anterior part of the hand, on the Kalatharee Sen. You can apply gentle tapping on the thenar and hypothenar eminences. The double consecutive taps generally leave a very pleasant feeling there.

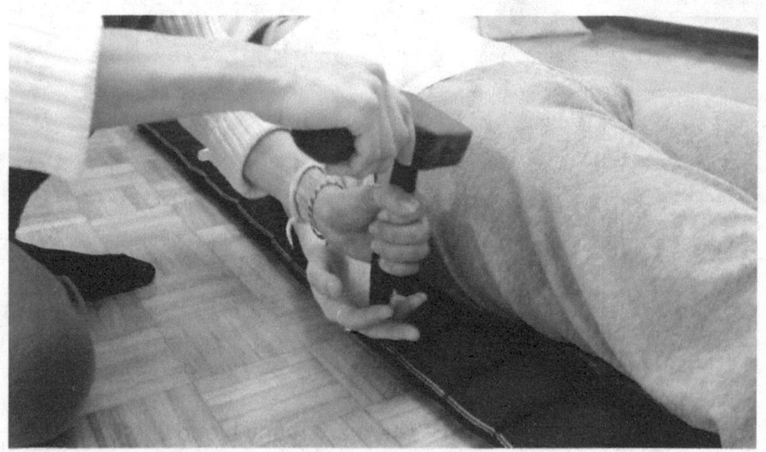

When working on the fingers, apply again feather tapping.

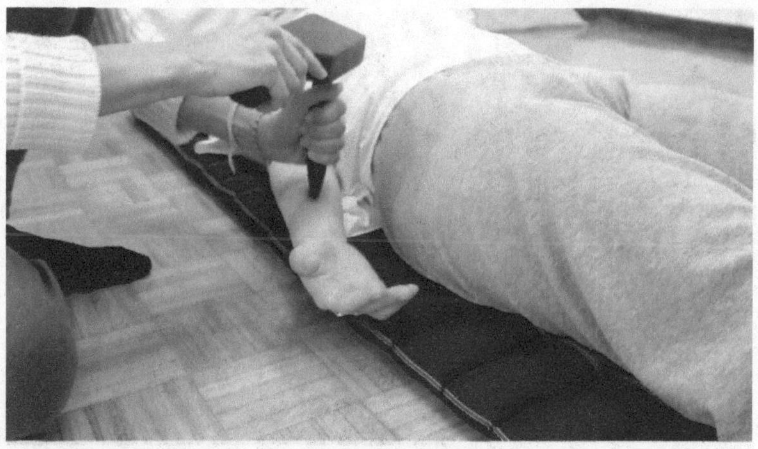

Then, work with tapping on the forearm.

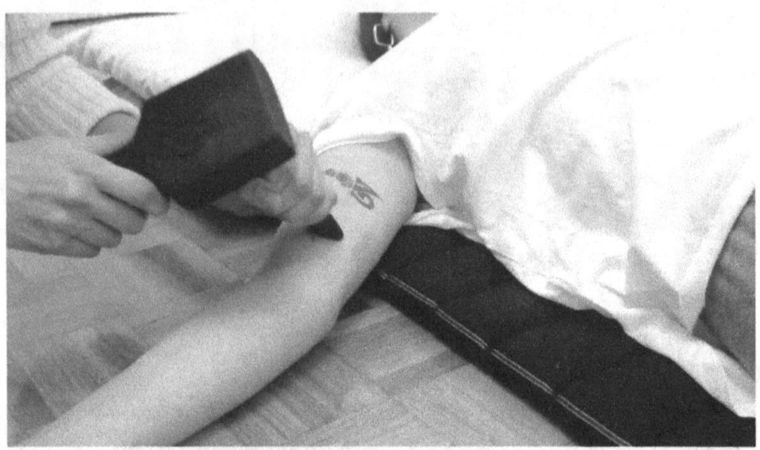

Tap lightly on the upper arm – there are many blood vessels in this area. Actually, we are tapping there mainly for "energy" reasons – just to tap on the Kalatharee sen line.

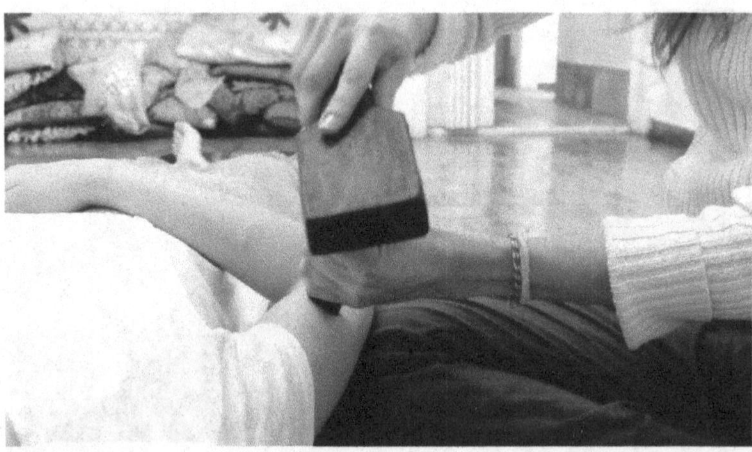

When you reach the elbow, bend the arm and place it on your thigh (this is recommended for mat-based bodyworkers – if you are working on a massage table, just place a pillow below the elbow joint).

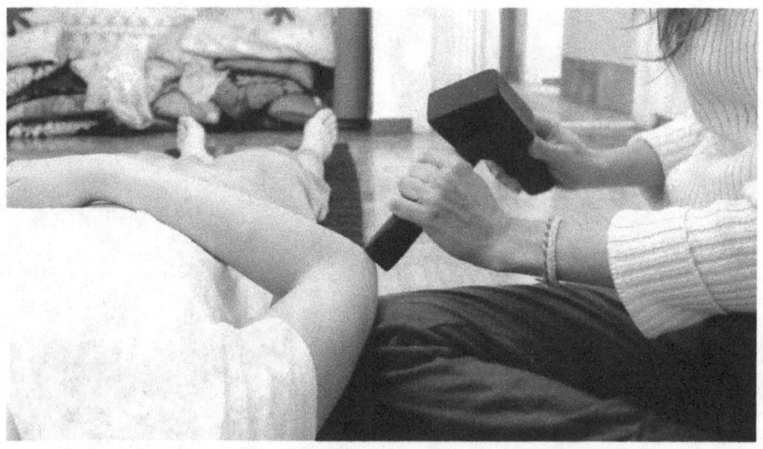

Do circular "feather tapping" around the elbow joint. You can perform "cross friction" on any painful or inflamed areas with the Tok Sen tools. Be VERY gentle, as the muscles are quite delicate in this area.

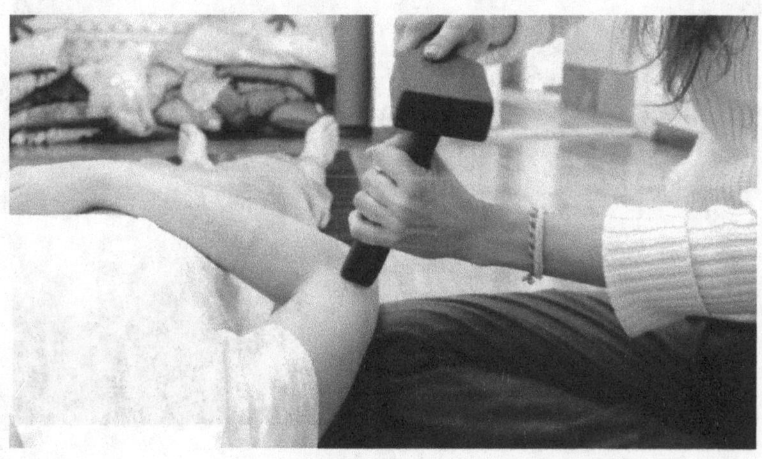

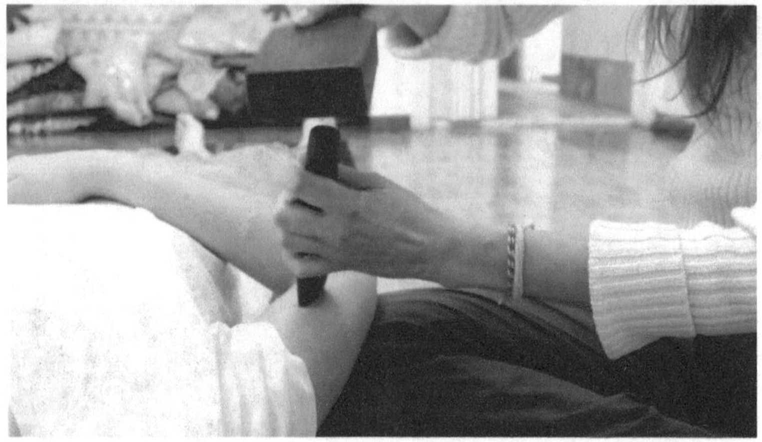

Maintaining the arm in the previous position, work upwards, following the Itha & Pingkala branch on the upper arm. Again, be very gentle. It is not necessary to do feather tapping – just tap lightly...

...Then work again downwards, towards the elbow...

... and then move upwards, towards the shoulder joint.

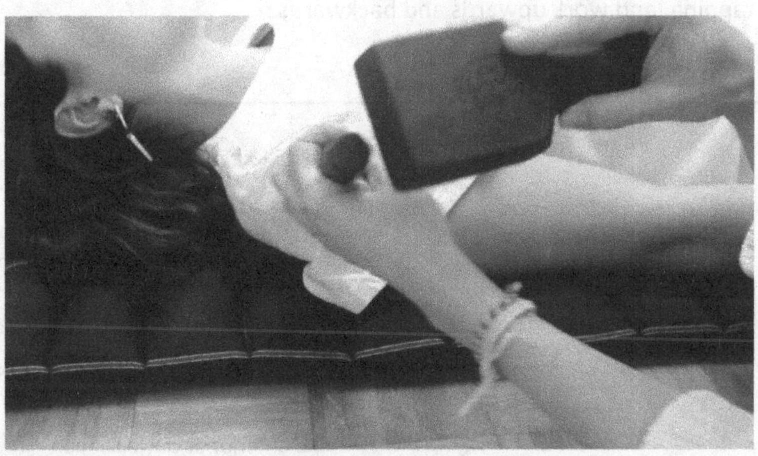

When you reach the shoulder joint, you have the option to perform feather tapping close to the joint.

You can even work ON the joint, if you are very careful. In that case, work in a spiral, in a really fast pace so that you do not hit any bones (the humerus or the clavicle).

This is a good moment to work on the deltoid muscle.
You can work between the three heads of the muscle. Apply gentle
tapping, and work upwards and backwards.

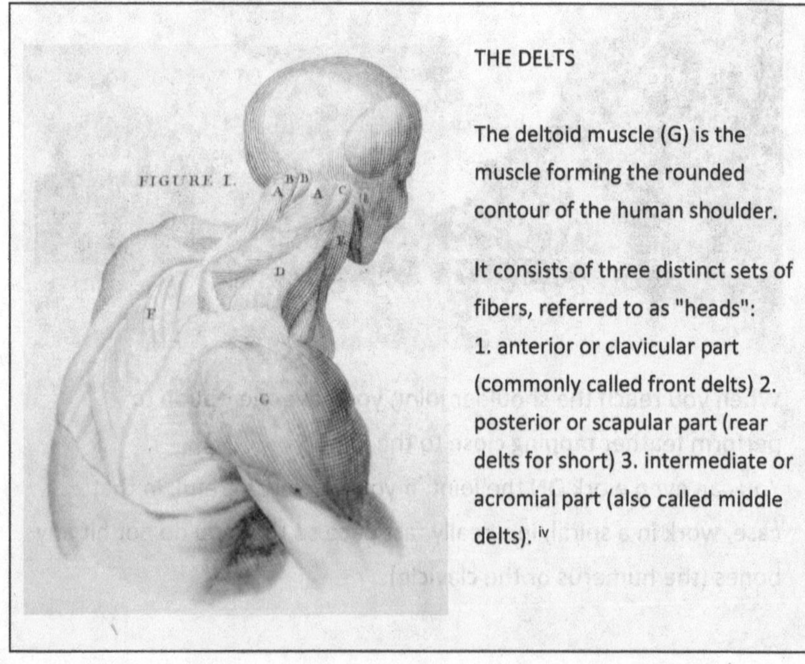

THE DELTS

The deltoid muscle (G) is the muscle forming the rounded contour of the human shoulder.

It consists of three distinct sets of fibers, referred to as "heads":
1. anterior or clavicular part (commonly called front delts) 2. posterior or scapular part (rear delts for short) 3. intermediate or acromial part (also called middle delts). [iv]

Conclude this part of the session by tapping on a very important point of the Kalatharee Sen. The point is on the upper lateral chest, above the acromioscapula, in the depression below the acromial end of the clavicle.

This point is indicated for any type of chronic cough and stress. After tapping on it gently 5-6 times, you can massage it with your index and middle fingers, applying light circular friction.

The application of hot herbal balls (luk pra kob) on this point, is also recommended.

PATTERNS OF TAPPING FLOW

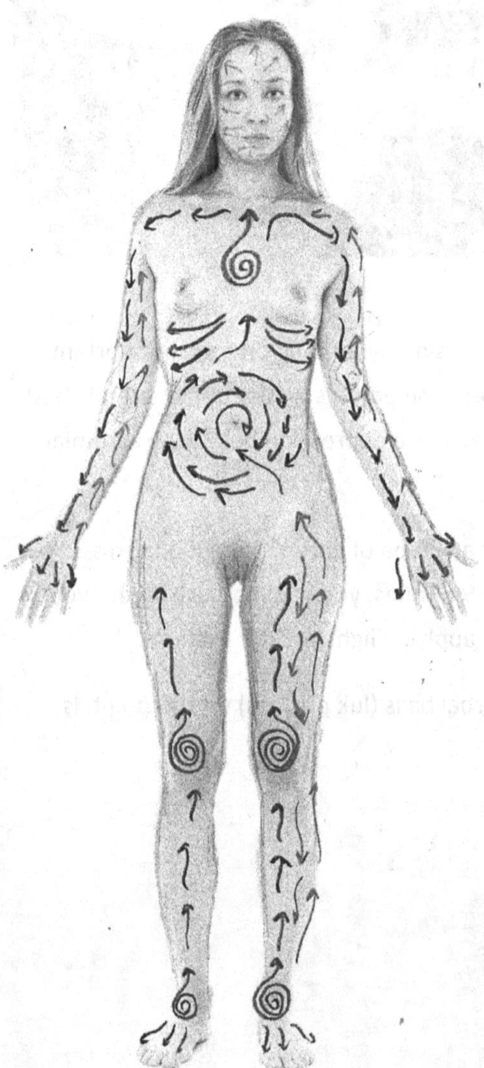

This is an example of a Tok Sen tapping flow on the anterior aspect of the body.

It is possible to tap on an entire side of the body (not at the face), and then cover the other side. When working on an entire side, the therapist can tap upwards and downwards on the Sen lines of this area.

Of course, Tok Sen can also be applied topically and / or separately on each limb and on the trunk.

Side position

The side position is perhaps the most important position of Thai Massage, as it gives us the opportunity to work on the whole body.

Actually, a Tok Sen session can be comprised solely by the side position. Moreover, it is a very comfortable position for the receiver, especially for people with lower back problems, as it respects all the spinal curves. Another benefit of side-positioning is the increased accesibility.

Any technique applied to the one side of the body, should be applied on the other side too.

In this position, it is strongly recommended to combine Tok Sen tapping with massage, herbal packs and Thai balms.

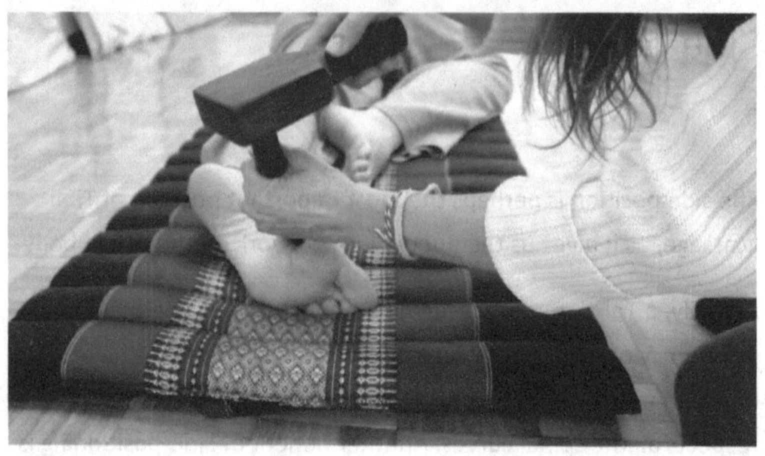

Start at the feet. Work on the Kalatharee Sen lines that are located there, at the plantar aspect of the foot.

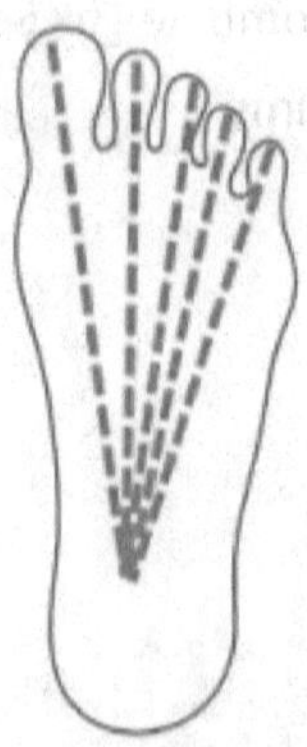

Do not apply tapping on the toe joints. Work from the big toe towards the pinky toe, on 5 lines. Start at the ankle, and work your way towards the toes, on the "paths" shown at the diagram.

Apply gentle tapping in this technique.

Work with feather tapping around the ankle. Cover the entire area, working with swift, light tapping. Repeat 3-4 times. Then, proceed to apply Tok Sen between the heads of the gastrocnemius muscle – that is, on the Itha & Pingkala Sen pathways.

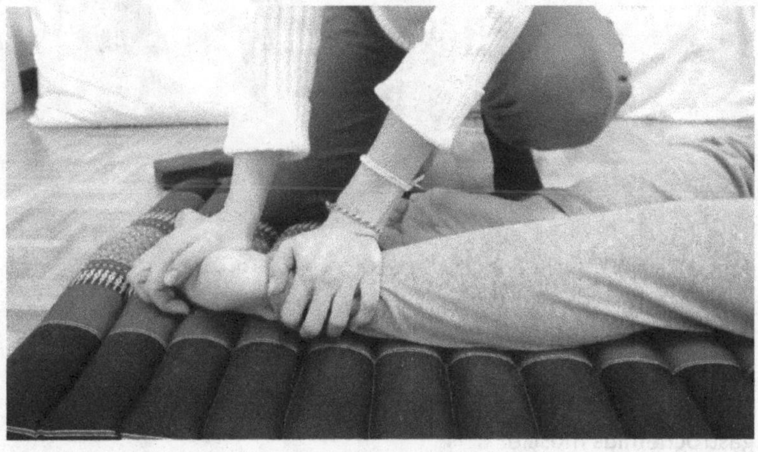

It is recommended to apply Thai Massage techniques between tok sen work. In that case, I am applying palm presses on the lower leg. I start at the foot, by doing 4-5 presses.

...then I continue with "butterfly presses" on the gastrocnemius muscle. Please skip the knee joint.

You can also do palm presses on only one head of the gastrocnemius muscle.

Another recommended technique is palm friction – in order to do this, apply circular friction on the gastrocnemius muscle with the thenar and hypothenar eminences. Repeat 3-4 times on each spot.

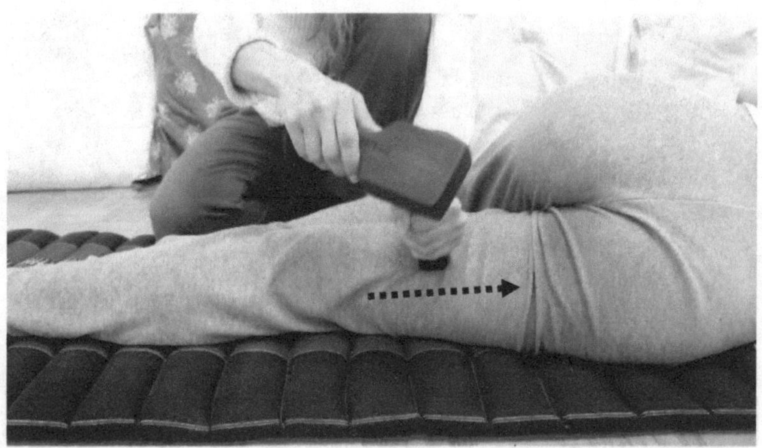

Then, proceed to work on the posterior aspect of the thigh. Do tapping on the Itha & Pingkala Sen lines – work 3 times, upwards and backwards.

You can work with a fairly strong tapping in this area. Be sure to skip the knee, and not to work on the gluteus muscle from this position.

Insist on this area if the client is suffering from sciatica or chronic lower back pain. After Tok Sen tapping, apply hot herbal packs with plenty of turmeric and ginger.

Perform tapping on the gluteus muscle. Avoid the sacrum and iliac bones. It is possible to apply stronger pressure in this area.

Work in the direction demonstrated on the photo. Repeat 4-5 times on each "line". Herbal packs are recommended for this area too.

If the client experiences knee pain, it is always a good idea to work on the tensor fascia latae, the iliotibial band, and the thigh adductors. And this position is ideal! Perform tapping on these structures – your pressure should be lighter compared to that which can be applied on the gluteus muscle.

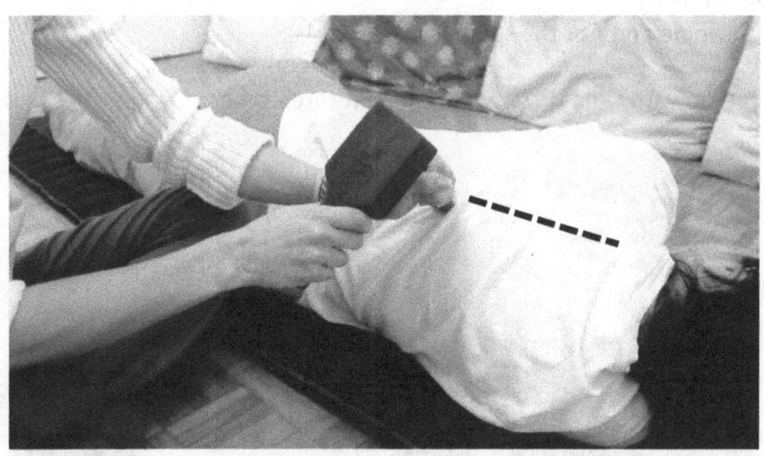

Time to work on the back! The truth is that it is preferable to work on the back when the client is at prone position.

However, it is not always possible to place the client at prone position. Thus, a massage therapist should be able to release muscular tension and correct imbalances from the side position as well.

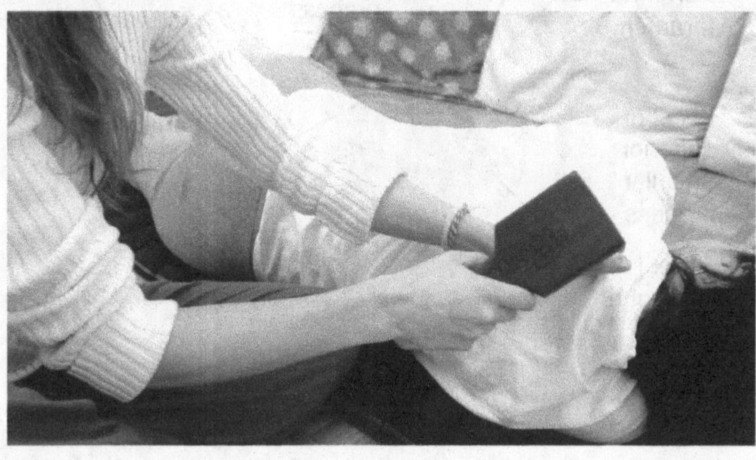

Work parallel to the spine. Perform tapping next to the transverse processes of the vertebrae. On no occasion should you ever tap on the spine and / or the spinous processes!

Tap upwards and downwards. Repeat three times.

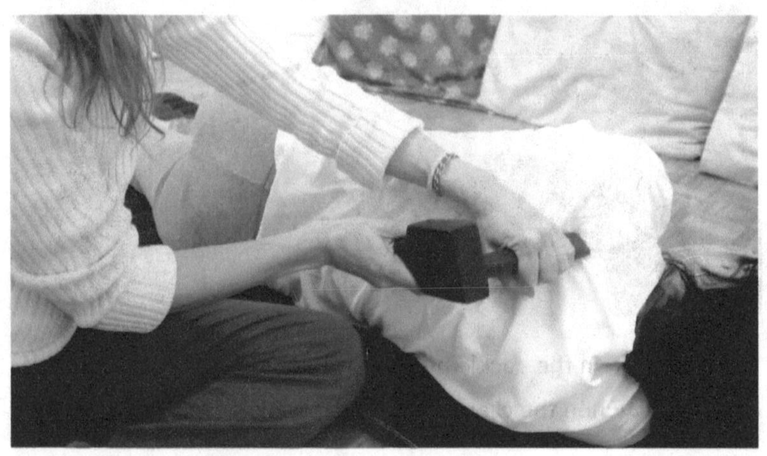

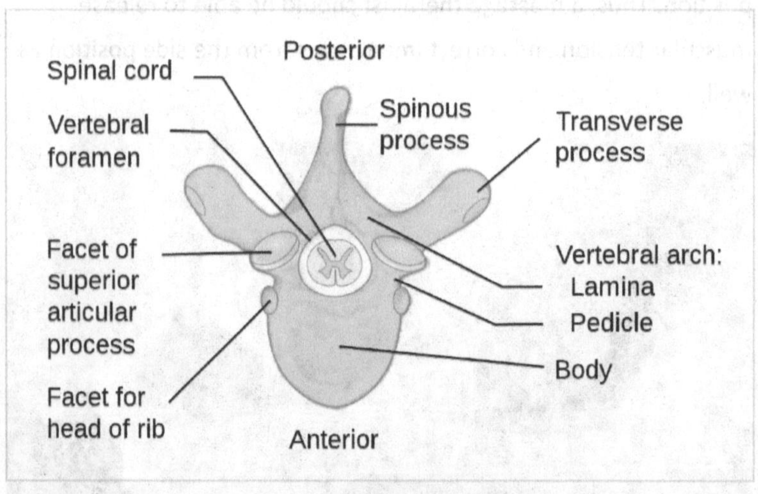

7. A superior view of a vertebra, with labelled description. ⁵

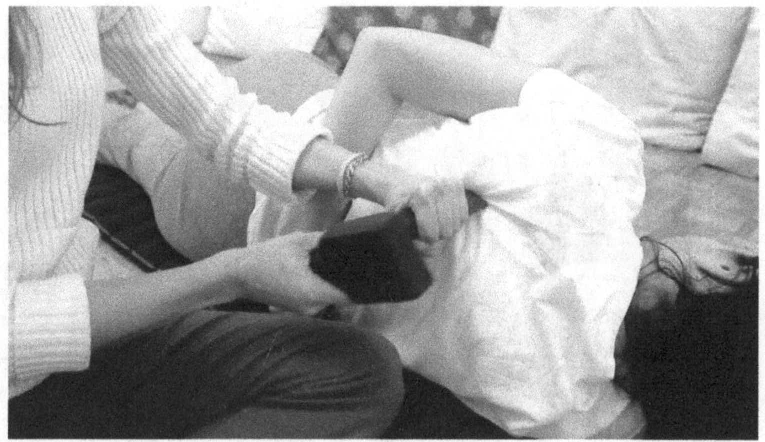

Place the client's arm behind the back, in order to access deeper layers of muscles, like the rhomboid muscles. Apply strong tapping there – it is always more pleasant (and less painful!) than it seems.

One caution: Actually, strong tapping should be applied only next to the medial border of the scapula. It will be painful (and even dangerous) to apply forceful tapping at the upper border of the scapula. There are many delicate muscles in the area.

Repeat 5-6 times, working upwards and downwards.

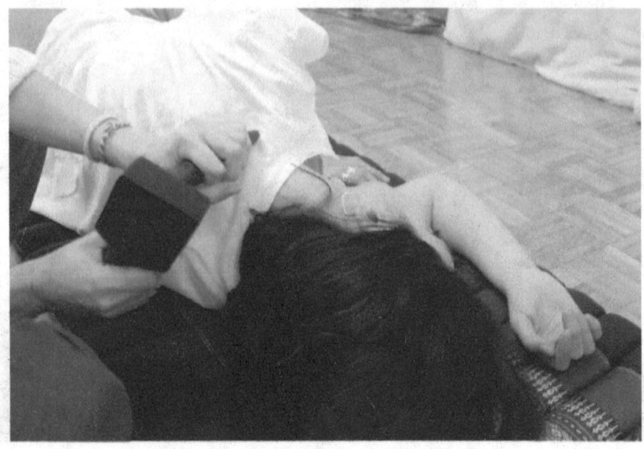

Apply gentle tapping above the superior border of the scapula. Stop before the coracoid process (this is the site of attachment of several muscles and ligaments, and thus should be avoided).

Repeat 4-5 times, at both directions.

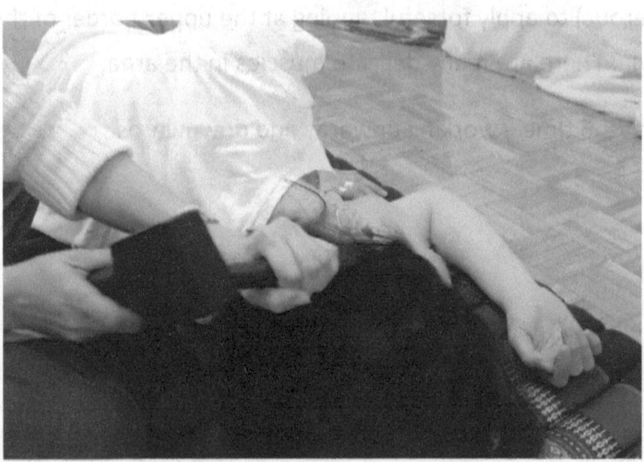

Apply feather tapping on the neck, avoiding the large blood vessels at the side of the neck. Tap until the base of the occipital bone, and work again downwards. Repeat 3-4 times, at both directions.

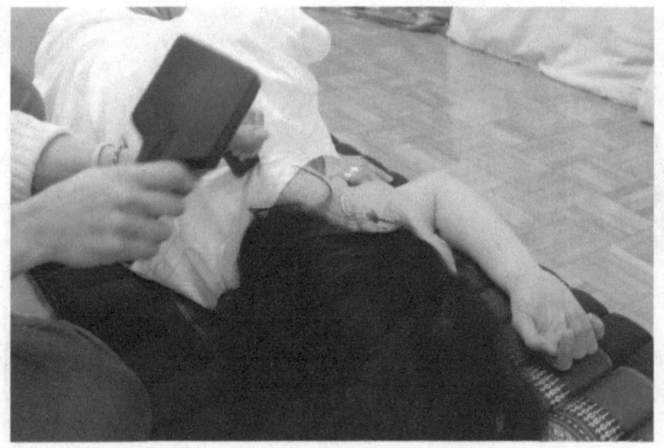

Return to the superior border of the scapula...

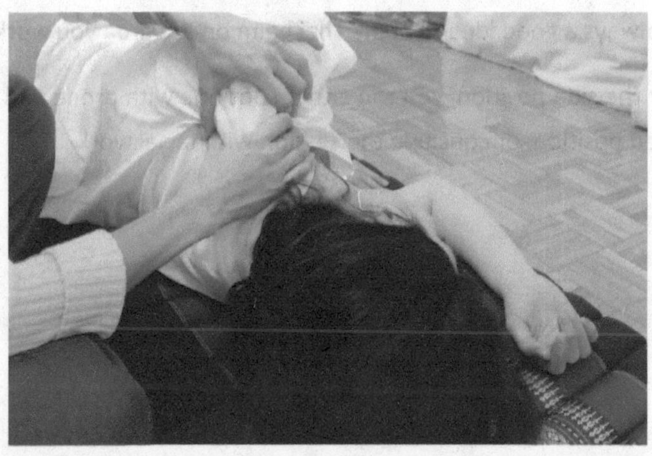

...and continue your work at the side position with massage on the shoulder area. Apply some decent kneading on the trapezius muscle, for about half a minute (or more)!

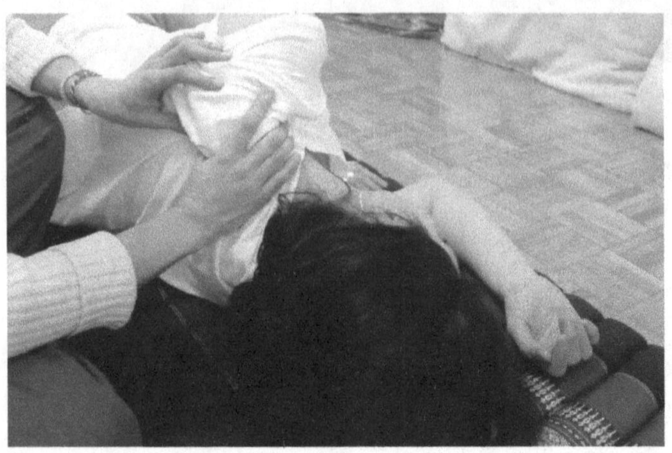

Conclude your work with acupressure around the scapula. Grab the shoulder, and do thumb presses on the rhomboid muscle.

It is always a good idea to apply Thai balm on the area you worked.

After the side position, you can either continue with prone and / or seated position, or conclude the session with facial work.

Prone position

Definetely, the prone position is the most relaxing massage position. In fact, most people have in mind the prone position when they hear the word "massage" – it is something like a synonym.

Prone position is of course, great for back and legs massage. You may need some pillows in order to support the receiver's body properly. You may have to place one pillow under the receiver's belly, in case of lumbar lordosis. Also, a headrest is always handy, because it supports properly the head and the neck, and facilitates work on the upper back.

Prone position is contraindicated in the following cases:

- After the first trimester of pregnancy
- In cases of serious respiratory disorders, like chronic obstructive pulmonary disease (COPD) , or even severe asthma.
- After heart surgery or bypass surgery. Prone position is also contraindicated for congestive heart failure (CHF).
- In very obese clients.
- In patients who suffer from severe sinusitis.

TAPPING FLOW ON THE BACK

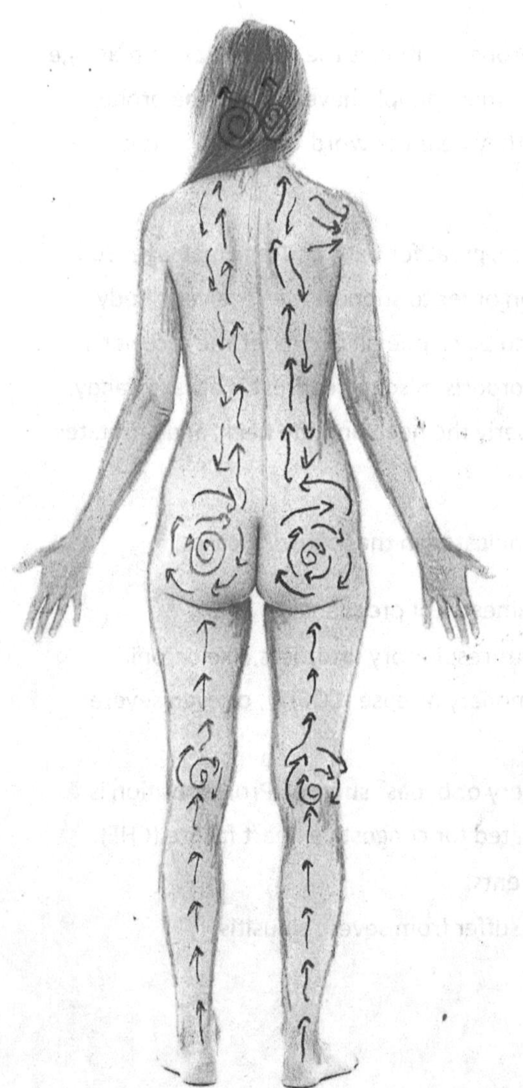

This is an example of a Tok Sen tapping flow on the back of the body.

It is possible to tap on an entire side of the body, and then cover the other side. When working on an entire side, the therapist can tap upwards and downwards on the Itha & Pingkala Sen lines of this area.

Of course, Tok Sen can also be applied topically and / or separately on each limb and on the back.

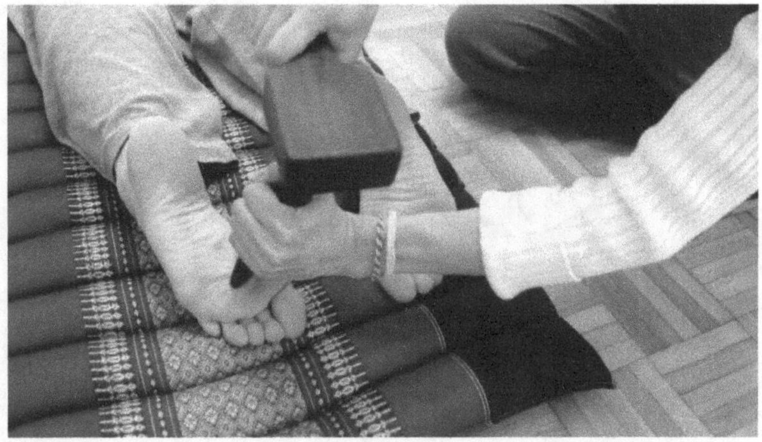

Start at the feet. Apply tapping with medium force on the soles. Cover the Kalatharee sen lines on the feet, avoiding any tapping on the toe joints.

Repeat 1-2 times, at a slow pace.

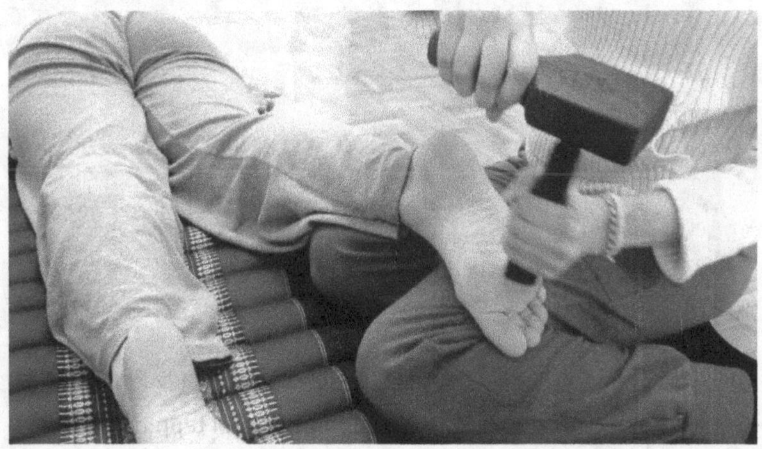

For a more comforting positioning, you can alternatively place the client's foot on your thighs. This could also slightly promote lymphatic drainage.

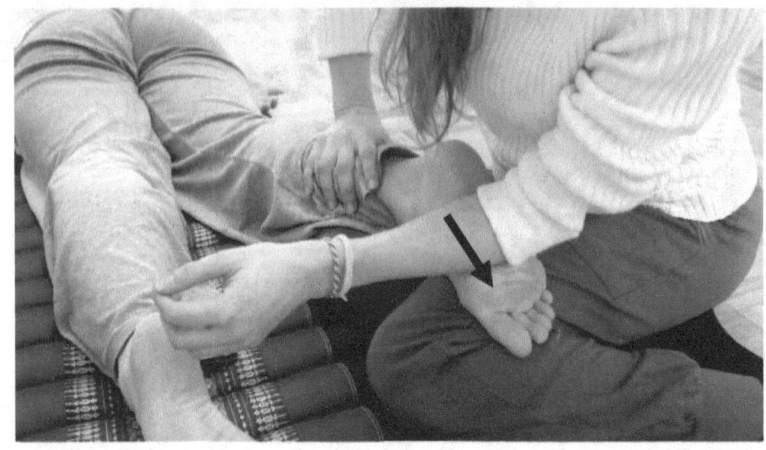

After tapping, roll your forearm on the foot, avoiding the toe joints. Repeat 4-5 times.

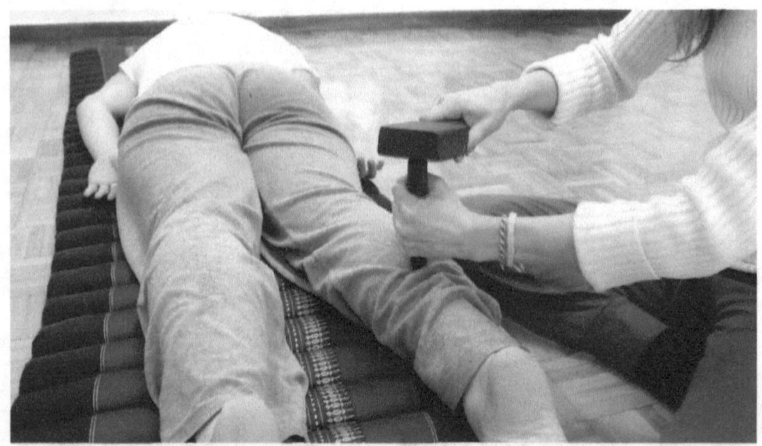

Then, proceed to the legs. Apply tapping on the Itha & Pingkala Sen, at the back of the legs. NEVER apply forceful tapping on the knee joint (it is actually better to avoid it altogether).

Focus your work between the heads of the gastrocnemius muscle.

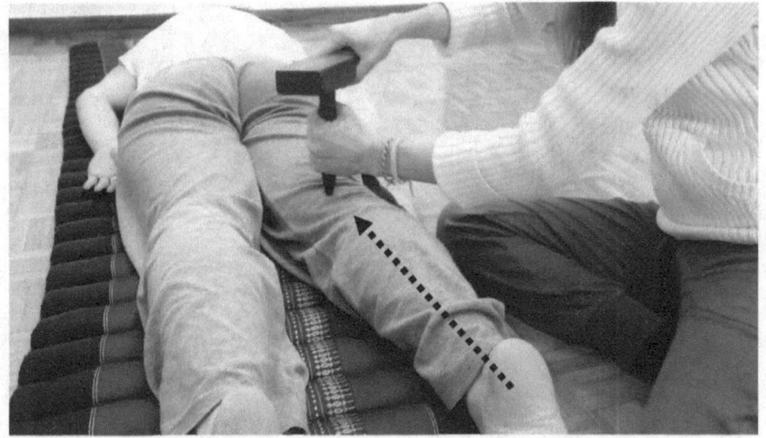

Work on the back of the legs, always tapping on the the Itha & Pingkala Sen lines. Stronger tapping is generally well tolerated in this area, and is recommended for muscle blockages.

Work upwards and then return to the feet. Repeat 2-3 times, always ending at the feet.

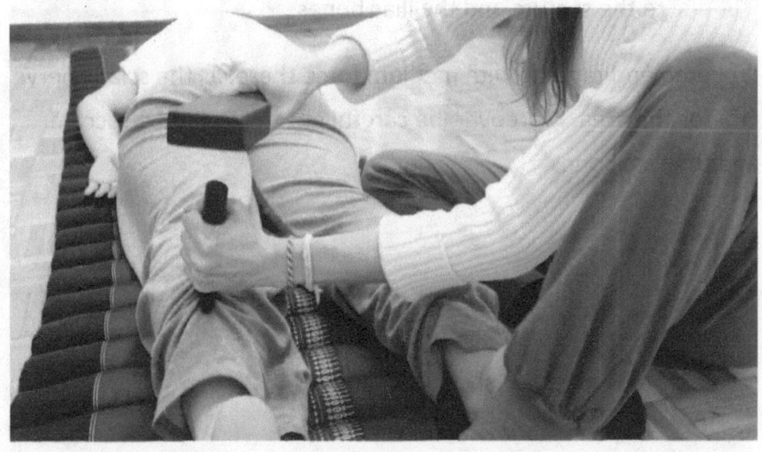

Then, repeat the techniques on the other leg, starting at the foot.

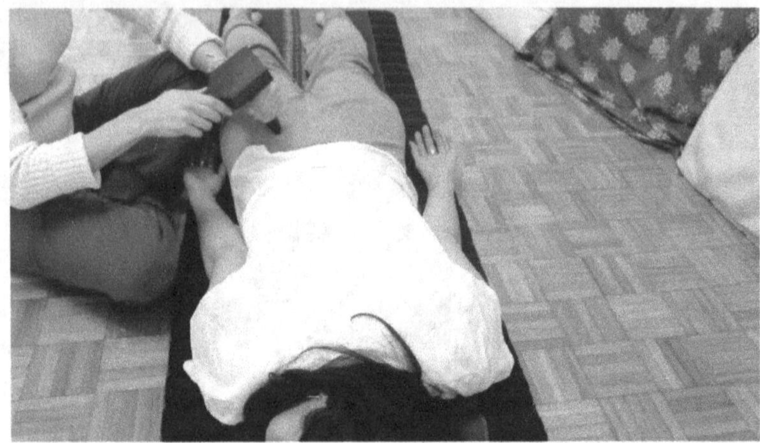

Perform tapping on the buttocks. It is possible to do that in various ways.

- You can tap around the sacrum and the iliac bones.
- In Thailand, I have seen therapists tapping the buttocks in a spiral-like pattern. That is, they start at the center of the buttocks, and then they "open" the spiral by tapping next to the sacrum and the iliac bones.

I recommend tapping with medium force there, as the sciatic nerve crosses the area. Moreover, be careful not to tap on the sacrum and the iliac bones.

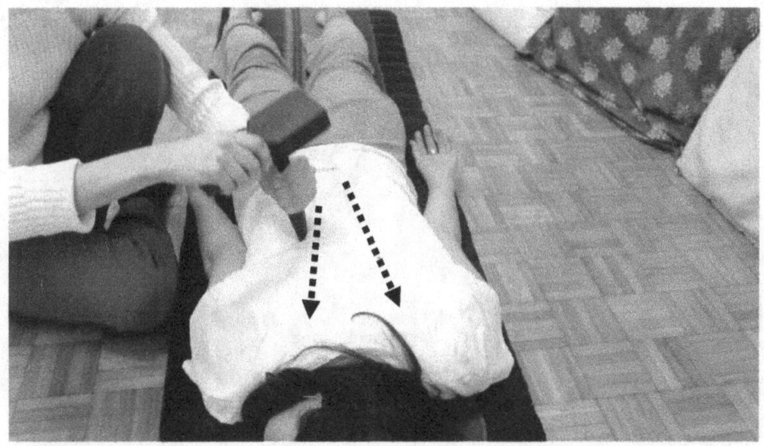

Tap next to the spine, following the course of Itha & Pingkala Sen lines. Tap lightly next to the lumbar region…

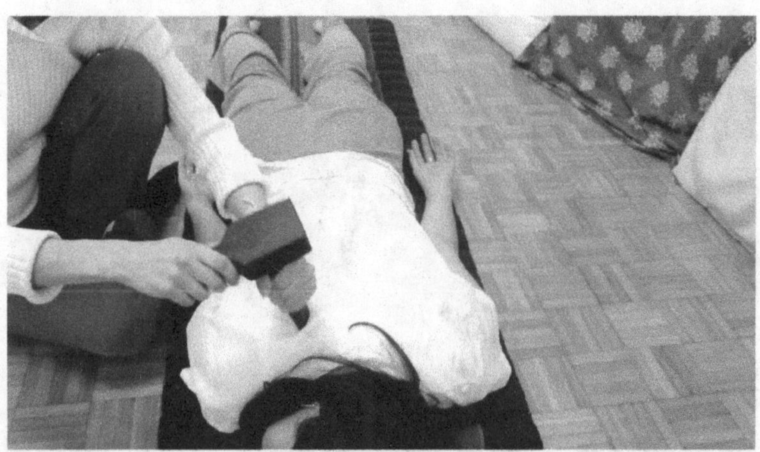

…and increase your force at the thoracic region. You may be scared from the sound, but do not worry: It just the air the lungs contain, which is responsible for that!

Proceed until the 2nd thoracic vertebra, and then return to the lower back.

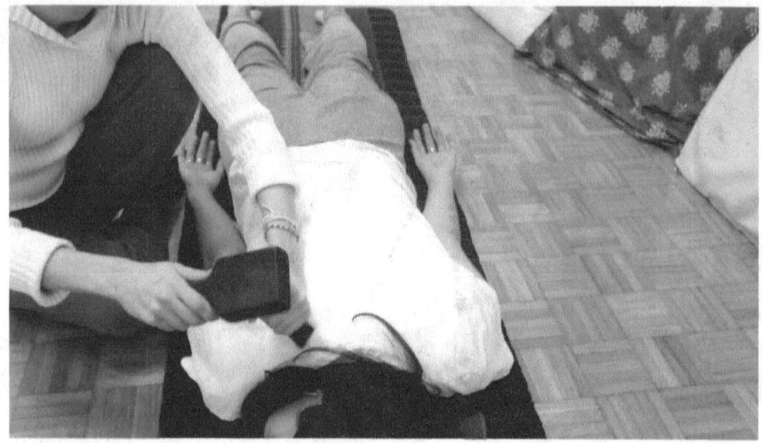

If your client is tense at the neck and / or shoulder region, you can focus more at the area next to the scapula. Apply forceful tapping and move upwards and downwards, about 10 times.

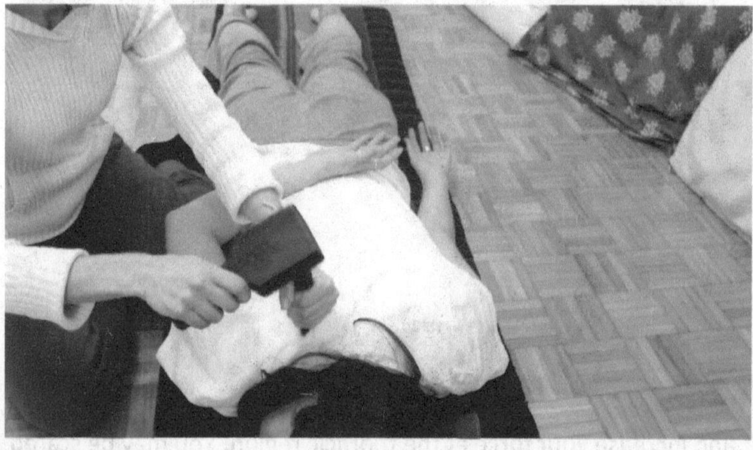

In order to access deeper layers of muscles, bring the client's arm behind the back, as shown in the photo, and tap next to the scapula.

Support the arm either by placing it on your thigh, or on a pillow.

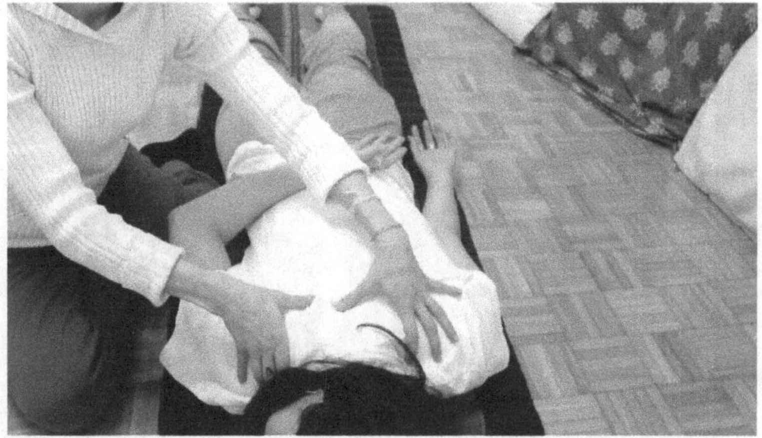

You can also apply massage (kneading techniques), warm herbal balls and thai balms. Then, proceed at your Tok Sen session at the other side of the back...

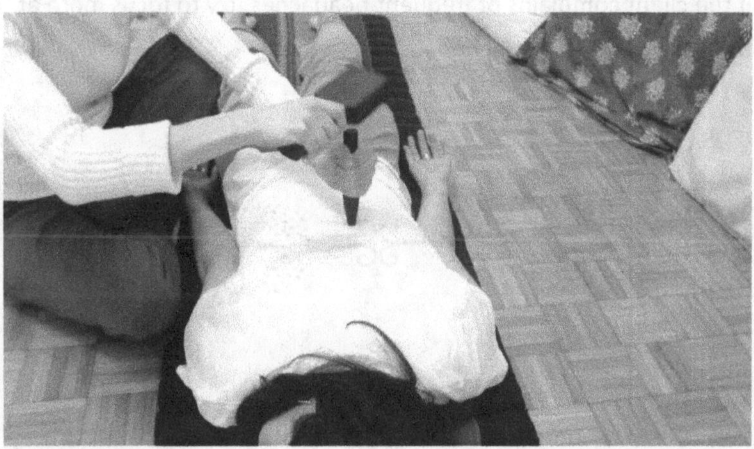

Repeat the previous steps, and conclude your work on the upper back with kneading.

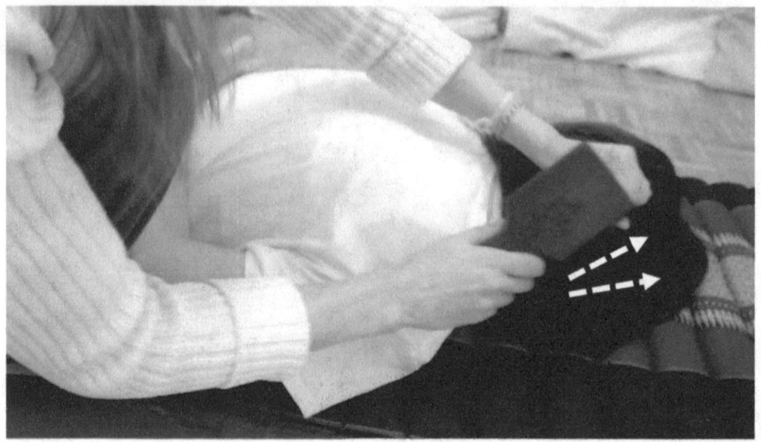

It is possible to do feather tapping on the scalp. Follow the Itha & Pingkala Sen lines, and tap VERY lightly the entire scalp.

Do not apply tapping at all on the neck, from this position.

If the client complains of frequent headaches, try to focus more at the base of the occipital bone.

This concludes the prone position techniques. Now we 'll see technique for the seated position.

Seated position

Seated position techniques are very effective for upper back, neck and shoulder pain. Of course, the downside of this position is that the client is not as relaxed as in prone or side position.

The recipient should be seated with his or her legs crossed. If this is not possible, he or she may sit on the mat with spread legs.

Tok Sen in seated position can also be applied as a stand-alone, quick treatment. It can also be incorporated in the typical Thai Massage seated position, or in seated position techniques of any type of bodywork. Plus, seated position is suited for pregnancy.

As always, Tok Sen is more efficient when combined with warm herbal packs and heat rubs.

It is best to skip the seated position if the client has had a recent lower back pain crisis.

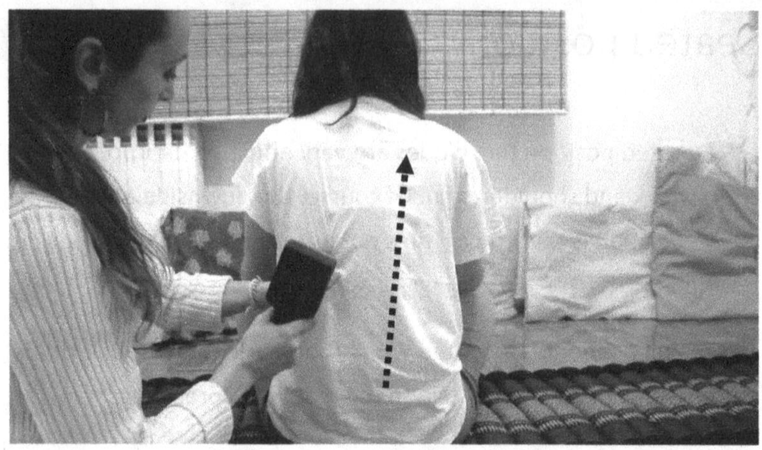

Tap on the Itha & Pingkala Sen lines. When tapping on the lower back, remember that the top of the iliac crests also marks the level of the fourth lumbar vertebral body (L4) – this is said because you should not perform tapping on any bones.

Medium force is recommended for the area of the lumbar spine.

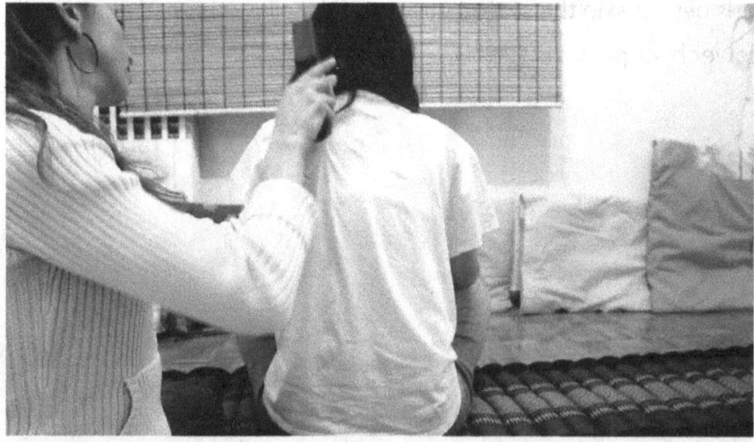

Proceed to the thoracic area. There, you can tap with greater force. Tap until the 2nd thoracic vertebrae, always working next to the spine.

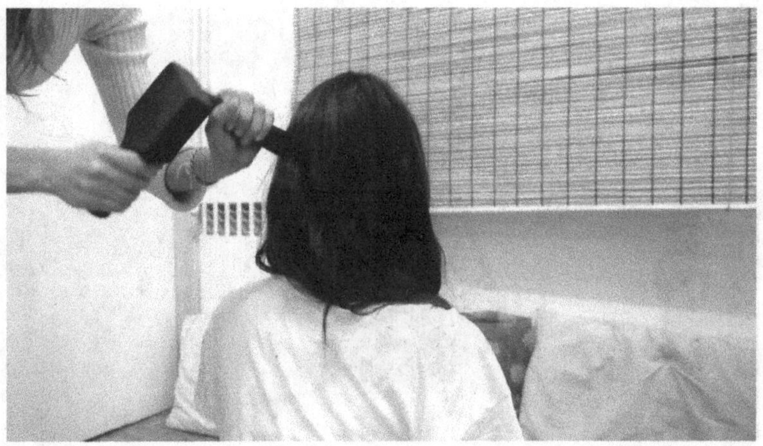

Do feather tapping on the scalp. Follow the Itha & Pingkala Sen lines, and tap VERY lightly the entire scalp.

Do not apply tapping at all on the neck, from this position. Actually, if you are going to work on the scalp at other positions, it is best to skip this altogether, because the client will not be relaxed.

In Thailand, I have seen therapists perform spiral-like patterns on the scalp, using the Tok Sen tools. This is very pleasant – moreover, spiral-like patterns can be seen at Thai manuscripts that depict traditional massage techniques and protocols.

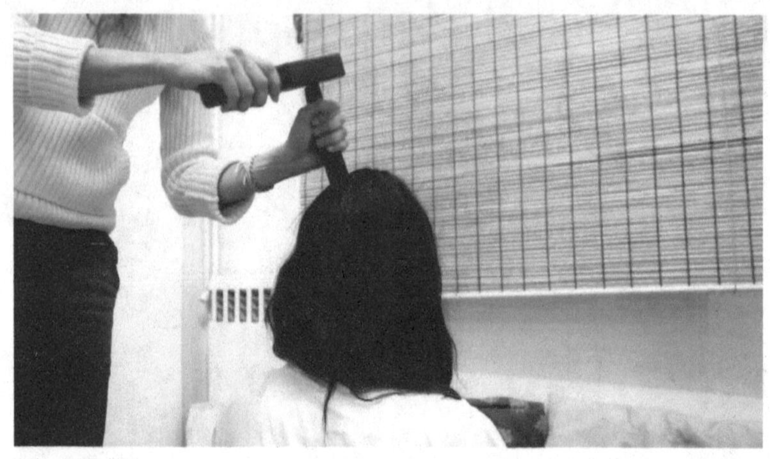

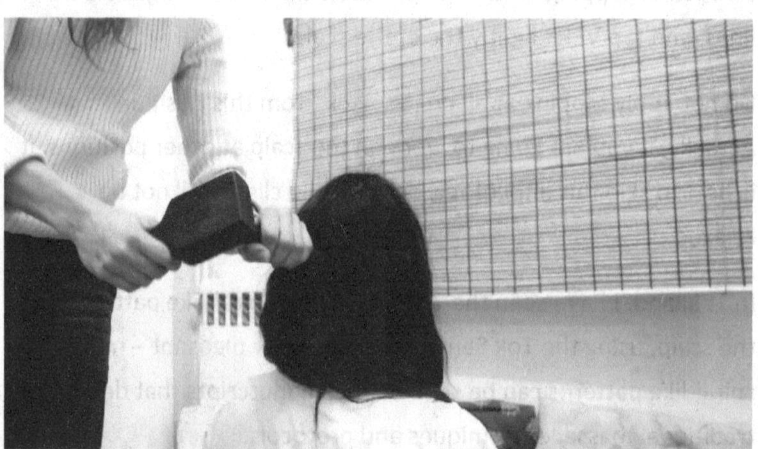

...And here's more tapping! Do not forget to tap lightly on the temporalis muscle.

And this concludes the (always short!) seated position.

Face

A Tok Sen session is concluded with face and scalp massage. These techniques are indicated for headaches, stress and neck pain.

It is recommended to apply them in the end of each and every treatment, since they help the receiver to calm down after the mobilizations.

Moreover, many Sen lines cross these areas – these include Itha & Pingkala Sen, Sahatsarangsi & Tawaree Sen, Lawusang & Ulanga Sen.

Work only with feather tapping on the face. I have found that only a highly skilled therapist can perform correct Tok Sen on the face. This is because feather tapping is performed at a quick pace, and this is generally undesirable for facial work. And this is where the skill is required: you have to apply feather tapping, and at the same time induce a relaxed feeling! As always, practice makes perfect - regular application is the only way to become proficient in it.

There are also many acupressure points on the head. Ideally, the adequately trained therapist should apply warm herbal packs on the forehead and the temples.

Before starting, you may want to cover the receiver with a warm blanket, and place a large pillow under his head, and one under his or her knees – this promotes the total relaxation of the spine.

These are some suggested patterns of tok sen tapping on the face.
Remember: only feather tapping is applied.

The tapping patterns on the face resemble the typical Swedish
massage ones: work upwards and outwards, following the shape of
the face.

Do not apply any oils and / or moisturizers.

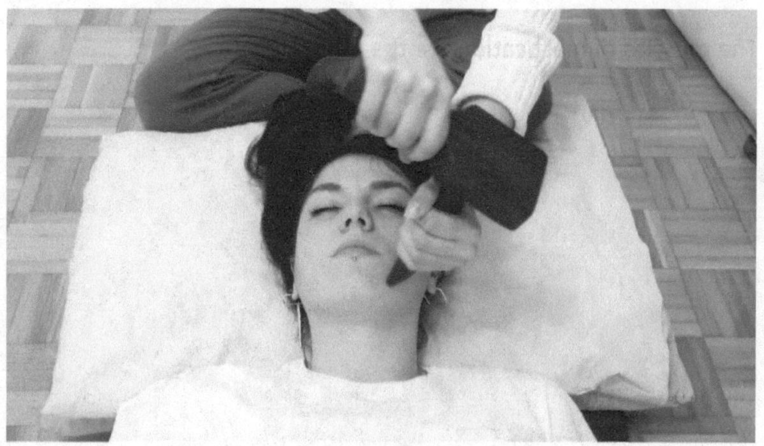

Start working from the jaw. Usually, there is a lot of tension there. Cover the entire area of the muscles of mastication.

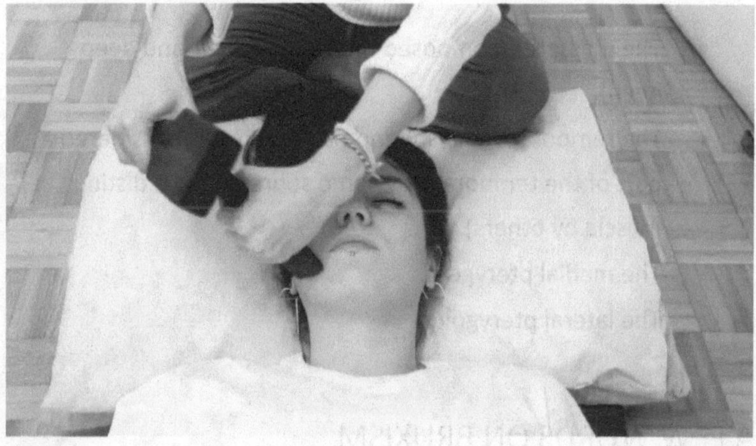

Repeat on the other side of the face.

This is recommended especially for people with bruxism – see next page for more information.

The muscles of mastication are the following:

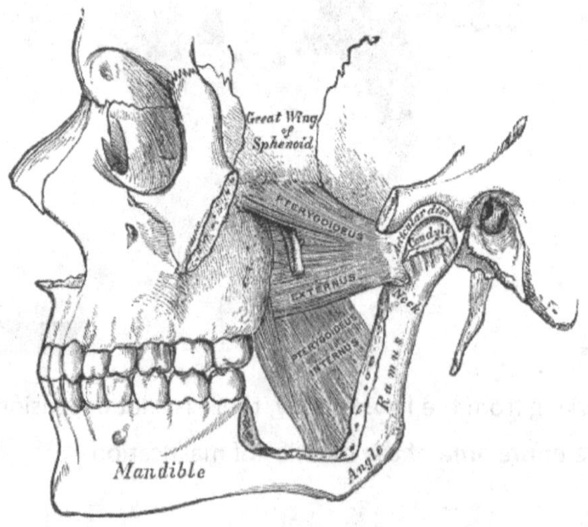

- The masseter (composed of the superficial and deep head).
- The temporalis (the sphenomandibularis is considered a part of the temporalis by some sources, and a distinct muscle by others).
- The medial pterygoid.
- The lateral pterygoid.

A FEW WORDS ON BRUXISM

Bruxism is defined as the excessive teeth grinding or jaw clenching. It is a common disorder; reports of prevalence range from 8% to 31% in the general population.

There are two main types of bruxism: one occurs during sleep (nocturnal bruxism) and one during wakefulness (awake bruxism). Awake bruxism is more common in women, whereas men and women are affected in equal proportions by sleep bruxism.

Several symptoms are commonly associated with bruxism, including hypersensitive teeth, aching jaw muscles, headaches, tooth wear, and damage to dental restorations (e.g. crowns and fillings).

Emotional stress and anxiety are the main triggering factors[vi]. Massage therapy and / or Tok Sen can be very beneficial for mild cases, since it can lessen the stress associated with this disorder. It can also promote the relaxation of the stiff muscles.

In cases of bruxism, always accompany Tok Sen work with massage on the entire face, and use warm herbal packs on the muscles of mastication. Additionally, work on the upper back, shoulders and neck, with Tok Sen and kneading. The application of intraoral work is always a great bonus, and should be used in that case by the properly trained therapist.

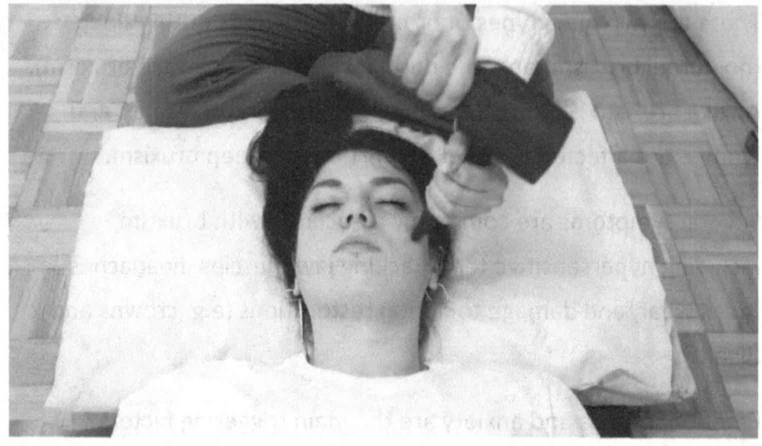

Work in the cheek area – the direction of your work should be from the nostrils towards the ears. Tap until the borders of the orbital area of the eye, and apply solely feather tapping.

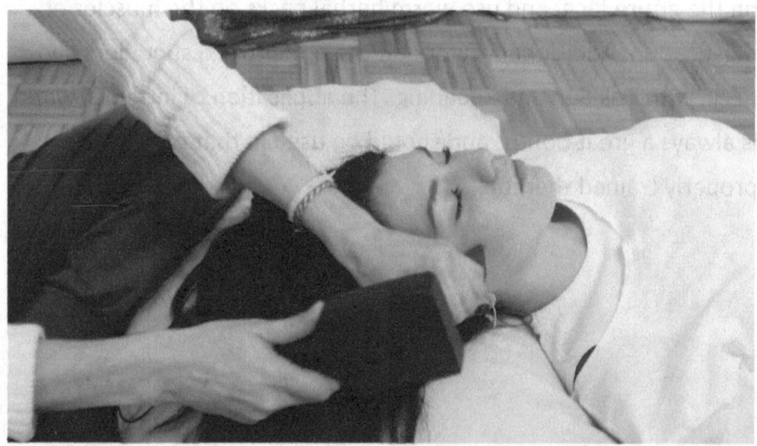

Repeat at the other side of the face.

Tapping on this area, as well as on the forehead can be beneficial for sinusitis.

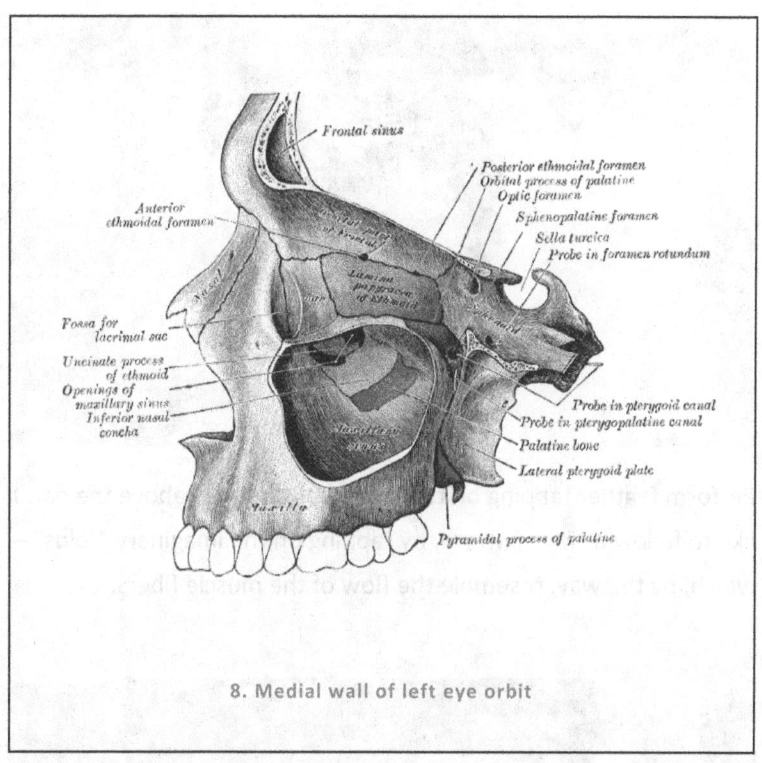

8. Medial wall of left eye orbit

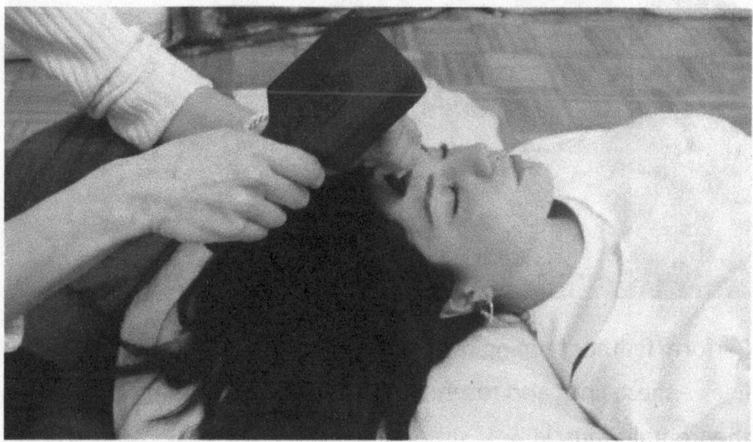

Apply feather tapping on the forehead. Work above the eyebrow, on the Itha & Pingkala Sen lines.

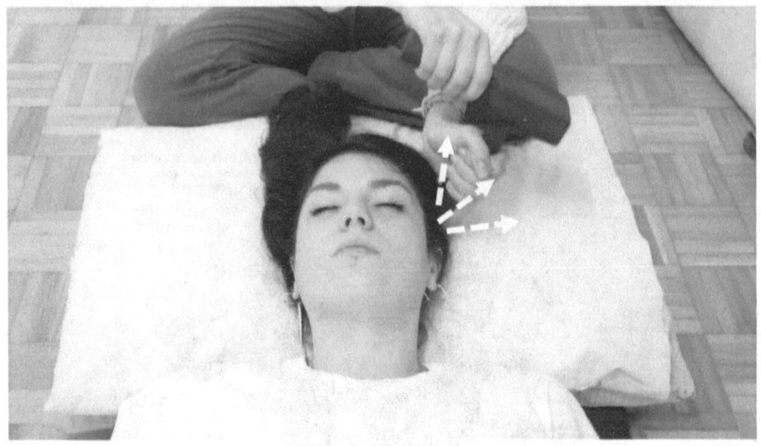

Perform feather tapping on the temporalis muscle, above the ear. I like to follow a "fan" pattern, by tapping on the imaginary "folds" – which, by the way, resemble the flow of the muscle fibers.

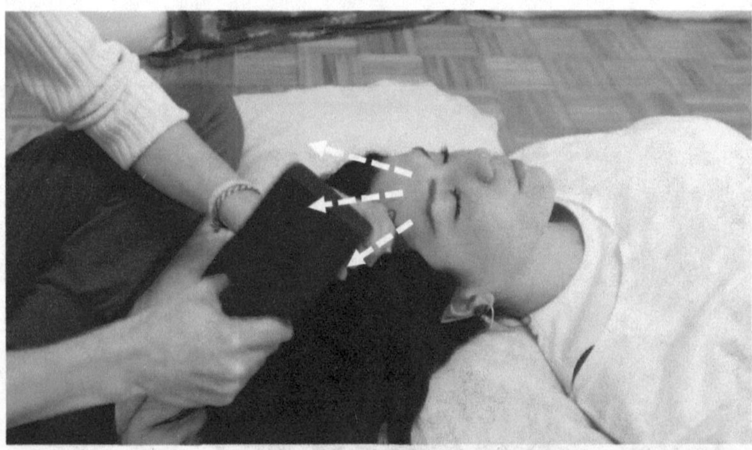

Perform feather tapping on the forehead, on imaginary vertical lines – these lines also resemble the flow of the muscle fibers of the frontalis muscle.

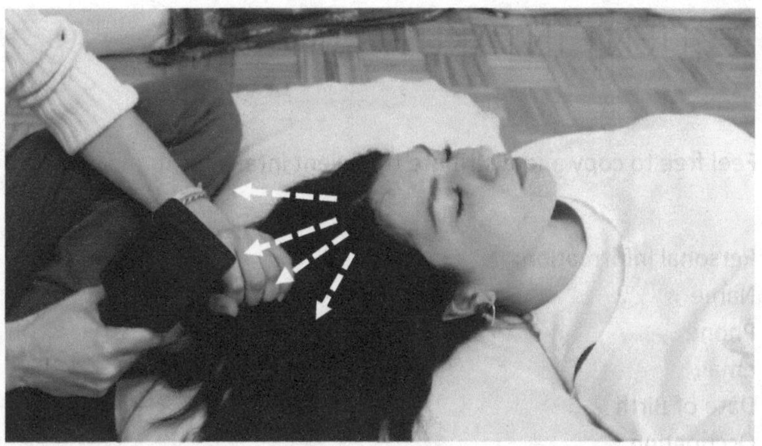

Applying the lightest feather tapping, work on the scalp. Work on imaginary vertical lines – these resemble the flow of the fibrous tissue of the epicranial aponeurosis.

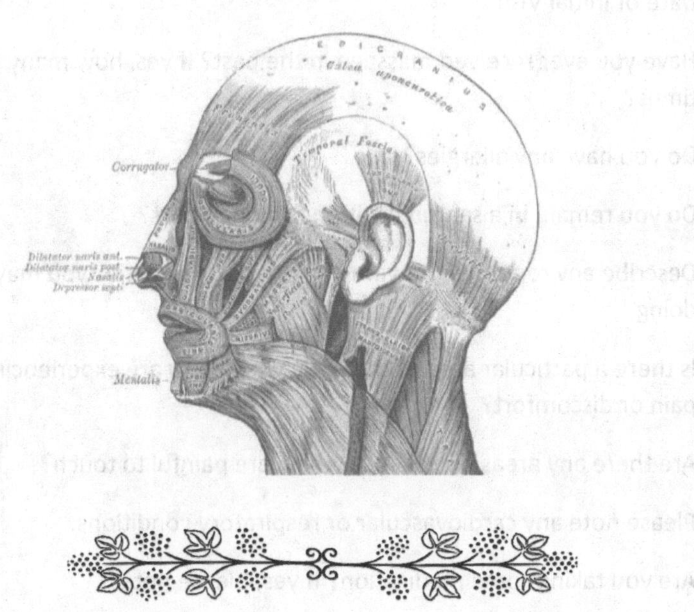

And this concludes the facial techniques.

A CLIENT INTAKE FORM

Feel free to copy and distribute this client intake form.

Personal Information:
Name
Phone
email
Date of Birth
Occupation
Emergency Contact Phone

Please answer the following questions to the best of your knowledge.

Date of Initial Visit

Have you ever received massage in the past? If yes, how many times?

Do you have any allergies?

Do you remain in a seated position for long hours?

Describe any repetitive movements or sports activities you may be doing.

Is there a particular area of the body where you are experiencing pain or discomfort?

Are there any areas on the foot which are painful to touch?

Please note any cardiovascular or respiratory conditions.

Are you taking some medication? If yes, please note it.

Do you have osteoporosis?

Are you pregnant?

Do you have any particular goals in mind for this foot massage session?

Is there anything else about your health history that you think your therapist should know?

The above information will allow us to offer you a safe treatment. Feel free to ask any questions about the information we request. All information will be kept confidential.

Therapist's name and signature

Client's name and signature

EPILOGUE

hope you liked this book. Please have in mind that it is a small budget production, and it was made mostly by one person – me!

The photos are actually screenshots from videos that were shot in my massage school, Flow – Wellness & Training, in Athens, Greece.

May these techniques be useful for your practice. If you have not attended a course, I hope it will inspire you to learn some type of massage therapy, tok sen and bodywork. This, I believe, is a sacred art, and it has a huge impact on one's character and life if practiced with sincerity and dedication.

One last thing: reviews are vital for all indie authors like me. Please leave a review for this book. Thank you!

ABOUT THE AUTHOR

My name is Elefteria Mantzorou. I was born in Athens, Greece. From my childhood I felt attracted to herbal medicine and alternative treatments.

Disregarding any common sense, and following the flow of events without any conscious decisions, I found myself in Thailand many times. There, I studied Thai Massage, Thai Foot Massage & Thai Herbal Compress at the Old Medicine Hospital, and at the school of the unforgettable Mama Lek and her son Jack Chaiya. I also met personally Tai Chi instructor, Tew Bunnag.

For several years I lived as a backpacker. I went to many places in Europe and Asia, working as a volunteer, studying, staying in ashrams, or simply traveling. I worked as a volunteer in wildlife sanctuaries, and have treated countless wild animals. In these sanctuaries, I also worked as a surgeon's assistant.

Another experience that has remained indelible in my memory is my acquaintance with Masanobu Fukuoka and natural farming, as I had volunteered in one of his projects in Greece.

In between my trips, I studied alternative medicine (aromatherapy, herbal medicine, Swedish massage and anatomy, physiology and pathology) and was certified as a medical translator. I also attended courses on osteopathy. I started teaching in 2004, and since then I have trained hundreds of people.

In 2013 I opened my own school, FLOW, in a quiet neighborhood of Athens. Well, until I start travelling again, you might find me somewhere here:

FLOW - Wellness & Training
8, Milona str., 11363 Athens
Website: jointheflow.net

Facebook: Flow – Wellness and Training
Instagram: @FlowAthens
YouTube: Flow – Wellness and Training

Newsletter: https://bit.ly/2lBLB1t

Be always well!

OTHER WORKS

You can see the other books I have published in Amazon here: amazon.com/author/elefteriamantzorou

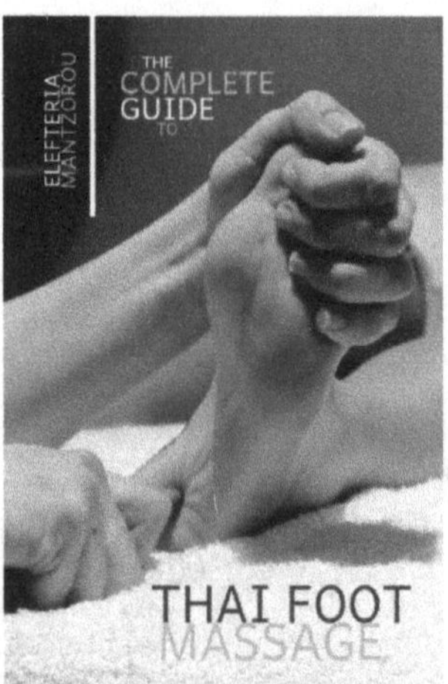

This book contains many techniques for the foot, the ankle and the lower leg, with detailed instructions.

Includes massage techniques with wooden reflexology tools.

Check out also the DVD "Thai Foot Massage", which includes the techniques of this book.

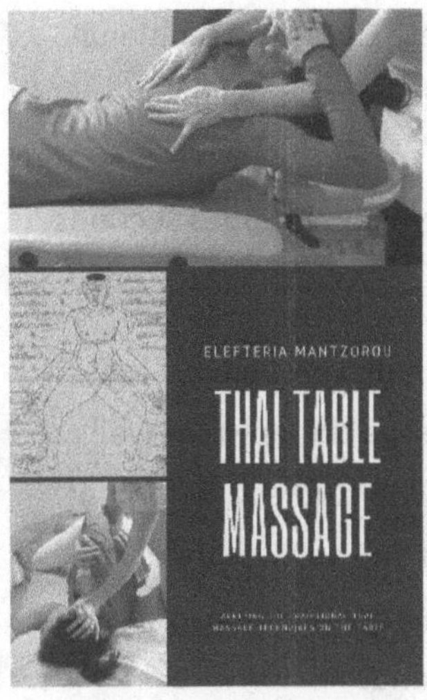

Learn to apply the traditional Thai Massage techniques on the massage table.

Take your massage therapy skills to the next level with Thai mobilizations.

The material of this book is also available in the DVD "Thai Table Massage", which is sold separately by Amazon.

 Master On Site - chair massage - techniques. Includes work with gua sha and bamboo tools.

The material of this book is also available in a DVD, which is sold separately by Amazon: "Professional Chair Massage".

The Complete Guide to Traditional Thai Massage contains valuable information about this ancient, sacred form of bodywork. Includes sections on Sip Sen.

This book is indispensable for the serious massage therapist, as well as for anyone who studies any form of bodywork. It will be also useful for those who simply wish to learn some massage techniques in order to apply them to family members and friends.

The material of this book is also available in a DVD, which is sold separately from Amazon, as "The Complete Guide to Thai Massage".

ENDNOTES

---

[i] Wikipedia.org
[ii] By Wikipedia commons. Credit: User Alifshinobi.
[iii] Wikipedia.org
[iv] Image source: University of Liverpool Faculty of Health.
[v] Source: user Jmarchn, Wikipedia.
[vi] Wikipedia.org

Photos of Tok Sen techniques, and all anatomy plates and diagrams
are created by Elefteria Mantzorou. All rights reserved.

www.ingramcontent.com/pod-product-compliance
Lightning Source LLC
Chambersburg PA
CBHW012041140726
47991CB00011B/3230